MW01622939

Neither Oldest Nor Best

How the Foundational Manuscripts of Modern Bible Translations are Fraudulent

David H. Sorenson

B.A., M. Div., D. Min.

Northstar Ministries
1820 W. Morgan St.
Duluth, MN 55811-1878

Northstar Ministries is a division of
Northstar Baptist Church, Duluth, MN

dhs.northstar@charter.net
http://www.northstarministries.com

Library of Congress Control Number: 2017900307
ISBN: 978-0-9711384-9-0

Table of Contents

CHAPTER ONE
INTRODUCTION

Why Another Book?

As the reader peruses this book, he or she might ask, why another book on this issue? There have been scores of books written on the Bible version or textual issue over the past 125 years. This author himself has contributed two such books. So why write and publish another book?

There are several answers to that question. First, information which has been long forgotten or covered up has again come to light in recent years. Second, with the advance of digital technology and high speed internet, scholars today have been able in very recent years to see remarkably clear reproductions of ancient manuscripts. These online digital photographs have allowed contemporary researchers to see details which many learned textual critics of the past 130 years were not able to see. Many of the notable and well-known textual critics of the past 130 years only saw crude facsimiles or printed transcriptions of the text of such well-known manuscripts such as Codex Vaticanus and Codex Sinaiticus. Yet in only the last few years, these foundational documents can now be seen anywhere in the world in precise detail.

> The term *codex* is a Latin word and refers to the binding of the pages of a book along its left side. It is the conventional way books have been assembled since about the 4th or 5th century A.D. The primary form of a "book" prior thereto was in the form of scrolls or a rolled up document. The volume of which you are reading is a codex style of publication. The term *codex* was thus used to distinguish documents produced in modern book form in distinction to the more ancient scroll type.

> The term *Vaticanus* refers to a major manuscript of the New Testament located in the Vatican library. It essentially means the book of the Vatican. Likewise, Sinaiticus refers to a major manuscript of the New Testament which was located at Mount Sinai. It similarly simply means the book of the Sinai.

Regarding long forgotten or covered up information, through the diligent efforts in recent years of men such as Chris Pinto and Bill Cooper, information which was widely reported and published in the 1860s has resurfaced. The essence of those allegations is that Codex

Sinaiticus is not an ancient manuscript of the New Testament, but rather was produced in about 1840 and subsequently doctored to look ancient. Needless to say, that allegation was controversial in the 1860s and certainly is so today. This author is certainly aware of the controversy and efforts to refute that allegation and discredit its sources. Yet, this author has studied the allegations and controversy carefully and believes that Codex Sinaiticus is indeed of recent origin and not dating to the fourth century — the conventional wisdom. Though this might seem to be a wild conspiratorial assertion, as we will see, there is very substantial evidence to verify these charges.

For a reader new to the subject, the manuscripts Codex Vaticanus and Codex Sinaiticus are the foundational sources of the modern Critical Text of the New Testament. And, the modern Critical Text is the text which underlies virtually all modern or contemporary Bible versions. Hence, we are dealing with issues which go to the foundation of the reliability and trustworthiness of modern Bible versions.

Likewise, through recently digitized photography of Codex Vaticanus, made available online, researchers can see the manuscript in detail previously viewed by a very few outside of Vatican scholars. That research has revealed that Vaticanus has clearly been doctored, edited, and even overwritten in many places thus neutralizing its integrity and reliability as an ancient representation of the New Testament.

Thus, as this book unfolds, the reader will come to realize that the modern Critical Text, which is the foundation of virtually all modern

Bible translations, is deeply flawed and is neither reliable nor trustworthy. The basic outworking of this is that modern or contemporary versions of the Bible are not reliable or trustworthy either.

That is a serious allegation. But that is what this book will demonstrate. That is why another book on the subject of Bible versions is necessary. The reader need not know Greek or really anything about Greek. This book rather is about one of the greatest deceptions in history — the counterfeiting of the Bible.

Diverse Readership

From many years of experience and having written several books on the Bible version/textual issue, I know this book will have a wide range of readers. For some, this will be their first exposure to the issue and they are thus newbies to the subject. Some will be sympathetic readers, some will not. In fact, some will be harshly critical. Some will be very knowledgeable on the issue with advanced degrees, some will not. I therefore will attempt to write to be helpful to all readers. As a long-time pastor and writer, my philosophy has generally been to put the jelly on a shelf where every one can reach it. Thus, the style of writing may be frustrating for those with advanced knowledge or those predisposed to be critical. But I long ago learned that books which are not easily understood are books which generally are not read to completion. They thus are not persuasive. Moreover, they are not well recommended nor do they sell well. Hence, though readers knowledgeable of this subject may consider the *style* of writing to be rudimentary, it is purposefully done that even the novice will understand. I beg the patience of the reader more advanced on this subject. But I will endeavor to present what often is technical and academic information in a way that all can grasp and understand.

Foundational Issue

After the publication and distribution of the book *Touch Not the Unclean Thing*, an individual called and said, don't you know the Greek says such and such. To which, I replied, "Which Greek?" This young, seminary-trained pastor did not know that there was more than one Greek text of the New Testament. Indeed there are two competing texts of the Greek New Testament.

On the one hand is the Traditional Text of the New Testament from whence the King James Version of the Bible is translated. On the other is the modern Critical Text from which is translated almost all modern and contemporary versions of the Bible, whether in English or some other language. Entire books have been written on the merits and demerits of each of these texts. We will endeavor to give a bit more insight into each of these in a following chapter.

However, the contention of this book is that the foundational documents of the Critical Text are neither reliable nor trustworthy. It therefore follows that the plethora of modern Bible versions are neither reliable nor trustworthy. Indeed, the integrity and veracity of the underlying text is a foundational issue.

As this book will unfold, it will become evident that both Codex Sinaiticus and Codex Vaticanus, the principal pillars of the Critical

Text, are deeply flawed and are not reliable. The corollary truth therefore follows that modern versions of the Bible based thereupon cannot be trusted. We are dealing with significant issues.

Basic Assertions

To reiterate that which was mentioned in passing above, the renowned manuscripts, Codex Sinaiticus and Codex Vaticanus, the principal essence of the modern Critical Text — are neither reliable nor trustworthy. As we will detail in coming chapters, Codex Sinaiticus was in fact produced between 1839 - 1840 in Greece by a Greek paleographer named Constantine Simonides. It is in reality not an ancient manuscript. Moreover, we will establish that it is riddled with problems and is one of the most corrupt manuscripts of the Greek New Testament in existence. This author certainly is not the first to advance this assertion. Moreover, voluminous efforts have been expended to discredit and debunk the claim that Simonides created Sinaiticus in 1840. However, we believe the evidence will prove Simonides' claim to be true.

Moreover, Codex Vaticanus, the other principle source of the Critical Text, claimed to be an ancient manuscript dating to the fourth century, likewise has major problems. As will be detailed later in this book, Vaticanus clearly has been doctored and modified by relatively recent hands. Those hands likely were in the Vatican and the changes made likely were done in medieval and even later times.

Hence, this book will proceed to show the validity of these two assertions: Sinaiticus is not ancient and Vaticanus was doctored, likely by Roman Catholic hands in more modern history. Thus, the very foundation of the modern Critical Text and its subsequent modern versions are neither reliable nor trustworthy.

CHAPTER TWO

OVERVIEW OF THE ISSUE

The Debate

The mention of New Testament textual sources seems arcane to most Christians. It has the musty odor of stale and dry scholarship. Yet, the text of the Greek New Testament is at the root of all the varying Bible versions. The difference between the NIV or the ESV or the NASB, for example, versus the King James Version is principally a textual difference. That is, the Greek text of modern Bibles is a different text than that of the venerable KJV.

A large majority of the fundamentalist movement uses the time-honored King James Version of the Bible. Virtually 100% of the broader evangelical movement uses anything but the King James Version. And, of course, liberal groups such as the National Council of Churches would not be caught dead using a King James Bible.

Needless to say, there is debate and controversy over which Bible is right. For the more liberal and evangelical movements, the choice of a Bible version is a smorgasbord approach. Every preacher, church, or individual chooses the Bible which seems right in his own eyes.

They pursue what suits their particular fancy. It is mainly the old, intractable fundamentalists which make an issue of the Bible. They overwhelming use the King James Version only.

Thus, there is division, controversy, and disagreement. Yet, for those who use the King James Version, there are principled reasons and much history. Once again, the issue goes to the underlying text of the New Testament.[1] Churches, Christian colleges, preachers, and scholars have divided themselves into two basic groups: those who stand on the King James Version and those who don't. But both views cannot be correct. One must be true and the other not. It is an either-or proposition and not a both-and one.

The issue is not petty. The integrity of the Bible is at stake. The advocates of the Critical Text and most modern Bible versions advance the notion that the King James movement lacks scholarship and is ignorant. Yet, there is great irony. In fact, it is the modern Bible crowd which is blissfully ignorant of recent research and the critical issues involved.

The Foundational Premise: Oldest is Best

At the core of the debate is the foundational premise that the oldest manuscripts of the New Testament are to be preferred to later ones. The logic is fairly simple. The oldest manuscripts will presumably be closer chronologically to the original text. They therefore will have suffered less textual degradation as scribes have copied and recopied the text over the centuries. Hence, the basic mantra of critical-textual studies is that the oldest is the best. Little regard is paid to what churches have used for centuries, even millennia. Nor is any credence given to the simple fact that Bibles which are continuously used wear out and are replaced. Hence, regularly used biblical texts are replaced with newer ones.

The same principle pertains to Greek manuscripts. Ones which were heavily used wore out and were replaced. The wore-out copies were burned ceremonially even as old flags are. Hence, the oldest copies used by churches long ago disappeared and only more recent copies exist. In contrast, manuscripts which have sat gathering dust in ancient libraries are prima facie evidence that they were never used and thus never wore out. Their antiquity is meaningless. To the contrary, it is evidence of documents set aside by the churches as aberrant copies to gather dust on forgotten shelves.

This author has aberrant Bibles in my personal library such as the Jehovah Witnesses' New World Translation. It is rarely if ever consulted and hence has no wear. It is a false Bible, but is in good physical condition. I, however, have sitting on my desk an old Scofield Reference Bible I used for many years in reading, teaching, and preaching. It is wore out and someday will be disposed of. Aberrant Bibles become old. Used Bibles wear out and are replaced. I likewise have an ancient copy of Young's Analytical Concordance given to me by my grandfather long ago. He used it regularly and I used it much in my early ministry. However, from much use, it is literally falling apart. Some day, it will sadly go to the place where old books die. In contrast, sitting on my library shelf is a set of commentaries I obtained new years ago. I have never used them and they remain in excellent condition.

The claim for Sinaiticus and Vaticanus is that they are considered to be the oldest extant (existing) largely intact copies of the New Testament and are therefore the best record of the New Testament. Therefore, modern scholarship weights them as being the most reliable source for ascertaining the text of the original New Testament. No one pauses to consider that books which have remained on the shelves of obscure libraries were never used by anyone. Being old is not any indication to the integrity of the text.

Nevertheless, most modern Bible versions of the New Testament are translated from the text based principally upon Vaticanus and Sinaiticus. They are considered the oldest and thus best. However, as this book will unfold, it will become evident that one is not old and the other was created or modified by relatively recent hands.

A Brief History of the Critical Text

Codex Vaticanus contributes the overwhelming majority of the modern Critical Text. The editors thereof departed reluctantly to Codex Sinaiticus for a lesser portion of the text.[2] The remaining very small percentage of sources derive from about 43 other "eclectic" texts.[3] There are more than 6,000 existing manuscripts of the Greek New Testament and more are waiting in the wings.[4] Thus, less than 1% of extant (existing) manuscripts support the Critical Text while approximately 99% support the Traditional Text. That in itself should be a telltale statistic.

But the principal manuscript source of the Critical Text is Codex Vaticanus (also known as "B"), from which the overwhelming majority of the modern Critical Text is based. Hence the Critical Text will largely rise or fall upon the integrity of Vaticanus — the book of the Vatican.

The Conventional History of Vaticanus

Let us therefore present the *conventional* wisdom and history of Vaticanus. Textual scholars from the mid 19th century onward have routinely dated it to the early fourth century A.D. Some textual scholars believe that what has come to be known as Vaticanus was one of 50 manuscripts commissioned by Constantine the Great in A.D. 331. Others discount that claim. But the basic claim is that Vaticanus is Alexandrian in its origins from the conventional history thereof. That is, it is presumed to have been produced by scribes at Alexandria, Egypt in the fourth century.

Alexandria, Egypt, at that time was the focal point of Gnosticism (a pseudo-Christian-pagan theological system) which did not believe that Jesus of Nazareth was the Christ. It is not the purpose of this book to delve into Gnosticism or the Gnostic impact upon the Alexandrian manuscripts.[5] But there is evidence that there was Gnostic influence in the production of Vaticanus.

There is no clear historical record of Codex Vaticanus (B) until it was registered in the Vatican library in 1475. It has been primarily housed there for as long as Vatican library records have been kept. In 1521, Erasmus of Rotterdam, through the Vatican librarian Bombasius, consulted it; but rejected it as corrupt and spurious.

Reconstruction of the Text

In the mid 19th century, the vogue of German Rationalism was the notion that the original text of the New Testament had been lost to antiquity. Therefore, men such as Constantine Tischendorf made it their mission to try and reconstruct the text of the New Testament by locating ancient manuscripts around the Mediterranean world.[6] It was for this purpose that Tischendorf visited the Vatican library in 1843 and was allowed to make a crude facsimile of a few verses of what came to be known as Vaticanus.

In 1860 eminent textual scholar Dean John Burgon of England was allowed to view the manuscript briefly. It should be noted the Burgon did not share the philosophy of Tischendorf in seeking to reconstruct the text of the New Testament. Burgon's conclusion was that Vaticanus was one of the most corrupt documents in existence. Burgon went on to assert that Vaticanus clearly exhibited a fabricated text — the result of arbitrary and reckless rescension.[7]

In 1867 Tischendorf was allowed to publish a transcribed edition of Vaticanus with the cooperation and permission of Roman Catholic Cardinal Angelo Mai. A transcribed edition is one that has been manually copied and then placed into print. This second-hand copy made its way to the renowned British Scholars B.F. Westcott and F. H. A. Hort. They in turn used it as the principal base of their coming revised Greek Text of the New Testament, first published in 1881. There is no evidence that Westcott and Hort themselves ever saw the actual codex, rather only transcribed copies or crude facsimiles. The Westcott and Hort Greek New Testament remains to this day the essence and base of the modern Critical Text.

The Conventional History of Codex Sinaiticus

The story of Sinaiticus is considerably more colorful and even convoluted. In 1844 Tischendorf visited St. Catherine's Greek Orthodox Monastery located at the foot of the traditional site of Mount Sinai in Egypt. In its disorganized and cluttered library, he claims that he found leaves of an ancient manuscript lying in a waste basket and being used as kindling for a stove. It is noteworthy that the monastery to this day denies this. In any event, Tischendorf claimed that the leaves he discovered were part of what would soon come to be known as Codex Sinaiticus. In due course, he claimed that he persuaded the monastery to allow him to take 43 leaves (86 pages) which he in fact did. These he deposited in the library of the University of Leipzig, Germany, of which he was connected. They remain there to this day.

Like Vaticanus, there is general consensus that Sinaiticus was originally produced in the 4th century and was of Alexandrian origins. It is also known as *Aleph* which is the first letter of the Hebrew alphabet.

In 1853, Tischendorf returned to St. Catherine's to retrieve the remainder of the manuscript but was rebuffed by the authorities of the monastery. Finally, in 1859, he returned again, this time with a story that he was acting under the patronage of Tsar Alexander II of Russia and on behalf of the Russian Orthodox Church, an adjunct of the Greek Orthodox Church. Tischendorf promised the leadership of the monastery that if they would loan the remainder of the manuscript to him, he would eventually return it. They acquiesced and loaned him the codex. However, Tischendorf never returned it and it seems that he had no intention of ever doing so.[8]

The remaining 344 leaves (688 pages) of the manuscript did go to Russia. Meanwhile, Tischendorf transcribed (i.e., manually copied) the text and then had it published in 1862. This facsimile also made its way to Drs. Westcott and Hort in London. They in turn immediately incorporated it into their ongoing project to produce a revised text of the New Testament. Sinaiticus and then Vaticanus became the basic backbone and gold standard of the modern Critical Text. Though it certainly has been tweaked and revised over the past 135 years, the modern Critical Text remains the basic work of Westcott and Hort. It is based principally upon Vaticanus and Sinaiticus. Again, there is no evidence that Westcott and Hort ever saw the actual physical pages of Sinaiticus, but rather only crude facsimiles or transcribed copies thereof.

Internal Problems of the Critical Text

What is ironic is that though Vaticanus and Sinaiticus are both considered to be of Alexandrian origin, they in fact are significantly different. There are thousands of places where the two manuscripts differ. In fact, Dean Burgon noted that it is easier to find verses in the two which do not agree with each other than which agree. There are thousands of words deleted when compared to the Traditional Text. There are dozens of verses missing in each. Perhaps one of the most egregious deletions is the last 12 verses of Mark which is a clear description of the resurrection of Christ.

Burgon wrote,

> "It matters nothing that they are discovered on careful scrutiny to differ essentially, not only from ninety-nine out of a hundred of the whole body of extant MSS. besides, but even from one another. In the gospels alone B (Vaticanus) is found to omit at least 2877 words; to add, 536, to substitute, 935; to transpose, 2098; to modify 1132 (in all 7578); - the corresponding figures for Aleph being 3455 omitted, 839 added, 1114 substituted, 2299 transposed, 1265 modified (in all 8972). And be it remembered that the omissions, additions, substitutions, transpositions, and modifications, are by no means the same in both. It is in fact easier to find two consecutive verses in which these two mss. differ the one from the other, than two consecutive verses in which they entirely agree."[9]

Burgon went on to write, "In the Gospels alone Vaticanus has 589 readings quite peculiar to itself, affecting 858 words while Aleph has 1,460 such readings, affecting 2,640 words."[10] These two manuscripts, which again would become the principal pillars of the modern Critical Text, are disparate to such a degree that they would be collated into one text borders on the absurd. Yet, the irrational acceptance of the "oldest is best" mantra blinds textual critics to common sense. The two differ in thousands of places.

Differences Between the Critical Text and the Traditional Text

I recently had a pastor tell me that when in college, a professor told him that there really is no difference between the various modern translations and the old King James Version. Such a statement reveals appalling ignorance. There are profound differences! When I was in seminary many years ago, a Greek professor informed the class that the differences between the modern Critical Text and the TR (i.e., Traditional Text), as he called it, would only occupy what might be the footnotes of one page in of a book. The fact is, that is wildly untrue. I suspect in each case, these ill-informed professors were merely repeating what a professor had taught them once upon a time. But they were categorically wrong.

The Critical Text omits more than 2,800 words when compared to the Traditional Text. That is the rough equivalent of I & II Peter. That is a huge difference. There are several dozen verses omitted entirely, and scores of phrases omitted.

Passages like the last twelve verses of Mark are usually found in modern translations, but are annotated in marginal notes that they are not found in the "oldest and best manuscripts." This thus questions one of the clear accounts of the resurrection of Christ in the Gospels.

Crucial words are changed. For example, in Luke 2:33 the traditional text speaks of the events following the birth of Jesus:

> "And Joseph and his mother marveled at those things which were spoken of him." However, The ESV which is a typical Critical Text translations read "and his <u>father</u> and his mother marveled at what was said about him."

The context clearly is of Joseph and Mary.

But virtually all other Critical Text translations refer to Joseph as the *father* of Jesus. That is absolute heresy and directly undercuts the doctrine of the Virgin Birth of Christ.

I John 5:7 is one of the clearest statements of the Trinity in the New Testament. "For there are three that bear record in heaven, the Father, the Word, and the Holy Ghost: and these three are one." However, Critical Text translations *delete* the final words of the verse: "the Father, the Word, and the Holy Ghost: and these three are one." This is an undermining of the doctrine of the Trinity. Moreover, I John 5:7 and its full reading is found in manuscript fragments of I John dating far earlier than Vaticanus or Sinaiticus.

Throughout the Critical Text of the New Testament, there is further diminution of the person of Jesus Christ. There are numerous disconnects of Jesus as Lord or Jesus as Christ. Though Jesus as Lord or Jesus as the Christ is not eliminated in the Critical Text, it certainly is diminished.[11] This should not be unexpected when one pauses to recount that Vaticanus, the principal manuscript underlying the Critical Text, likely was produced by scribes sympathetic to Gnostic philosophy and theology. Alexandria, Egypt, whence Vaticanus allegedly came, was the focus and locus of Gnostic influence in the fourth century.

Once again, among other things, Gnostic theology/philosophy did not believe that Jesus of Nazareth was the Christ. The numerous disconnects of Jesus as Christ or Jesus as Lord in the Critical Text therefore follow that opinion. The simple truth is that Gnostic scribes long ago either carelessly or purposefully altered the text of the New Testament to suit their theological bias.

Thus, there are many differences and serious alterations between the time-honored Traditional Text, manifested in the King James Version, and the Critical Text with its many concomitant translations.

Another major problem which pertains to the Critical Text is the theological associations and views of the various editors thereof across history. It is not the purpose of this book to delve into that area. But this author has already written several books detailing the theological liberalism, apostasy, and unbelief of virtually all of the editors associated with the Critical Text. Obviously, that is not a problem for many. But for a Bible believer, the editing, modifying, and revising of the New Testament at the hands of unbelieving editors is a major problem. Nevertheless, that is the case of the majority of the editors of the Critical Text.

The History of the Traditional Text

The focus of this book is not about the Traditional Text, but it is helpful to have a standard by which a comparison can be made. Recall that approximately 99% of extant (existing) New Testament manuscripts support or are parallel to the Traditional Text. And recall that the Traditional Text of the New Testament is that which has been used by almost all church groups down through the centuries with the exception of the Roman Catholic Church and liberal-leaning Protestants of the past 130 years. The Greek Orthodox Church, which still speaks the Greek tongue, uses the Traditional Text exclusively and never has used any other source. They know their own heritage and language.

There are several terms of the Traditional Text which are more or less synonymous. It has often been called the Received Text simply because virtually all groups, the Catholic Church excepted, received and used the Traditional Text until the latter part of the 19th century. The Latin term thereof is *Textus Receptus*. That at times is simply abbreviated to TR. Because many of the manuscripts of the Traditional Text came from the region of the Byzantine Empire, they are sometimes called Byzantine which is a reference to the Eastern Empire of the Greek Orthodox Church. Hence, the terms Traditional Text, Received Text, Textus Receptus, TR, and Byzantine Texts all are more or less synonymous.

A Different Paradigm

The paradigm or thought perspective of the Traditional Text, however, is substantially different from that of critical-text thinking. The critical-text mentality is to try and reconstruct the New Testament from the discovery of ancient manuscripts. They believe the original text of the New Testament has been lost to history and their mission is to try and reconstruct the text as new discoveries are made. Proponents of the Critical Text will freely admit to this day that they are unsure of the text and that it could change again tomorrow if new textual discoveries are found.

Hence, a popular manifestation of the modern Critical Text, the Nestle-Aland Text, is in its 28th edition. That is, the Nestle-Aland Text, which began essentially as the Westcott and Hort Text has gone through 28 editions. That means its text has been altered 28 times in the roughly 100 years it has existed. Though basically the text of Westcott and Hort, the Nestle-Aland editors have tweaked and modified it continuously for over a century.

However, the paradigm of the Traditional Text is completely different. It begins with the premise that the Word of God of the New Testament has never been lost and has been used by Bible-believing churches down through the centuries. Moreover, proponents of the Traditional Text believe that God has providentially preserved His Word. In fact, the Bible clearly discusses how that God will preserve not only His Word in general, but the very words thereof.

For example, in Matthew 24:35 Jesus said, “Heaven and earth shall pass away, but my words shall not pass away.” It is significant that Jesus did not say His Word would not pass away, but that His *words* would not pass away. The Bible clearly says that God will preserve the very *words* of Scripture. That is verbal preservation.

Morever, in Matthew 5:18, Jesus said, “Till heaven and earth pass, one jot or one tittle shall in no wise pass from the law, till all be fulfilled.” As most students of Scripture know, a *jot* was the smallest character or letter of the Hebrew alphabet. A *tittle* was a little horn of a Hebrew letter, sort of like the “foot” of a capital E in distinction to a capital F which does not have such a “foot.” (That may not be a precise illustration, but most readers will get the idea.) The greater point is that even the letters of the words of Scripture and even the very construction of the letters will not pass away. That clearly foretells the verbal preservation of the Word of God. If the very constituent parts of the words are preserved, the words themselves certainly will be.

Therefore, proponents of the Traditional Text are not running around looking for the latest discovery of manuscript fragments to ascertain what the Bible really says. We believe we already have the preserved Word of God in the Traditional Text. (And the major English-language manifestation thereof is the King James Version.) All we need to do is consider which text Bible-believing churches have used over the centuries. Invariably, the evidence will point to the Traditional Text.

Hence, a focus of the Traditional Text is not so much upon manuscript evidence, but upon *translational* evidence. The question thus arises, is there translational evidence of the Traditional Text in early church history? The answer to that is a resounding *yes*.

The Peshitta Translation

The Peshitta Translation is a Syrian (Syriac) translation of the New Testament. The word *peshitta* is a Syrian word which essentially means "simple" or "basic." To this day, it is considered to be the basic version of the New Testament of the Syrian Church. There is little or no dispute that it follows the Traditional Text. The dispute arises as to *when* it was first produced. The conventional wisdom is that the Peshitta Translation was made in the fifth century. However, Edward Hills, Ph.D., conclusively showed that the Peshitta was not produced in the fifth century A.D., but much earlier.[12]

Even F.H.A. Hort conceded that the Peshitta, which he called the Syriac, followed the Traditional Text. However, he like others tried to ascribe it to the fifth century. To place it earlier would destroy his own theory.

Of further note is that the Syrian Church to this day forcefully asserts that the Peshitta was *always* the New Testament of the Syrian Church. The Catholicus Patriarch of the Church of East, Mar Eshai Shimum asserted in 1957 that "the Peshitta is the text of the Church of the East which has come down from the Biblical times without any change or revision."[13]

Other sources indicate that the Peshitta was in fact translated in A.D. 150 by the Syrian churches whose principal church at that time was the Church at Antioch.[14] What is remarkable about that is A.D. 150 is about 55 years after the death of the Apostle John and less than 85 years after the death of the Apostle Paul. Moreover, the Church at Antioch was the home church of the Apostle Paul during most of his missionary ventures. Once again, the Peshitta Translation follows the Traditional Text. At that early date, the base source for the translation may have been in some cases original copies of New Testament books or at least first-generation copies thereof. This is powerful evidence of the primacy of the Traditional Text and that it is in fact the preserved Word of God.

The Italic Translation

The Italic Translation was produced in the year A.D. 157 in northern Italy by a group of churches called the Italic Church. They had no connection with the yet-to-develop Roman Catholic Church. The later Waldensian churches considered the Italic Church to be their ancestor and claimed a direct lineage from them. The Italic Translation also follows the Traditional Text. What is apparent is that the Traditional Text of the New Testament was used by churches in northern Italy as early as A.D. 157. This is clear translational evidence of the usage of the Traditional Text in the earliest years of Christianity.[15]

The Gallic and Celtic Translations

The Gallic Church existed in what today would be called southern Francc.[16] They produced a translation of the New Testament in A.D. 177 which follows the Traditional Text. The Celtic churches of Great Britain came on the scene in the latter part of the second century and used a Traditional Text translation of the New Testament.[17]

The Gothic Version

In A.D. 350, a missionary to the Germanic Gothic tribes of central Europe by the name of Ulfilas produced a translation of the New Testament on the field. It is known as the Gothic Version. It also parallels the distinctives of the Traditional Text. Ulfilas translated his work while laboring in Bulgaria. There is a copy of it at the University of Uppsala in Sweden to this day. However, for our purposes, what is particularly significant is that a missionary on the field, in a remote place, without access to libraries or other helps, produced a translation of the New Testament from a source which parallels the Traditional Received Text. What is clearly implicit is that the Traditional Text was the working text of the churches of that era. Once again, there is translational evidence of the primacy and antiquity of the Traditional Text.

Other European Bibles

The Greek Orthodox Church has used the Traditional Text continuously since the fourth century when it split from Rome. In actuality, it used the Traditional Text even earlier. Martin Luther's German Bible used the Traditional Text, as did the Olivetan French Bible, the Diodati Italian Bible, and the Spanish Reina Valera, to name a few. Though the Greek Orthodox are really not orthodox in all of their doctrine, the Waldenses who produced the Olivetan Bible certainly were as was Giovanni Diodati, one of the Swiss reformers. Then there was the Tyndale Bible, the Geneva Bible, and the Czech Version — they all used the Traditional Text.

The Overwhelming Stature of the King James Bible

The principal translation of the Traditional Text in English has been the King James Version. Indeed, over the past century, there have been other English-language translations of the Traditional Text. I am often asked, could there be a new translation of the Traditional Text into English? In fact, in recent decades, several English translations of the Traditional Text have been published. However, none of them have enjoyed wide distribution.[18] To be more blunt, they have all flopped.

The Spanish language has enjoyed the Reina Valera Bible, which even predates the KJV. Up until recently, most editions of the Reina Valera have been based upon the Traditional Text. The Reina Valera Bible is probably the second largest language translation of the Bible in history. Yet, its distribution is just a fraction of the distribution of the KJV.

The King James Bible, first published in 1611 has dominated the distribution of the Bible ever since. According to British historian Adam Nicolson, more than five *billion* copies of the KJV have been printed and distributed over the past 400 years. In fact, the British Society of the United Kingdom estimates the number to be over six *billion.*[19] That is more than any other Bible version in history. That likely is more than all the rest put together. The reader might pause and contemplate the assertion just made. The most widely distributed version of the Bible in all of history is the King James Version.

Though the Latin Vulgate has existed since the fourth century, it was (a) in Latin which few except the Roman clergy could read and most of them did not read it. (b) It was only hand copied into the middle ages. And, (c) thereafter, it again remained a Latin version of the Bible which few read and relatively few were published in the greater scope of Bible publishing.

The simple fact is that no other version or translation of the Bible comes close to the King James Version in its publication and distribution. More copies of the King James Version of the Word of God have been printed and distributed than any other Bible in all of history. I will reiterate the assertion that more copies of the King

James Bible likely have been printed than all other versions in all other languages put together.

Now, that is either a coincidence and a fluke of history, or God has had something to do with that. I am of the opinion that the publication and distribution of the most widely used version of the Word of God in history is not a coincidence. God in one way or the other very likely had something to do with that.

And that brings us back to the basic issue of which text is the true text of the New Testament. Moreover, in the century preceding the advent of the KJV, the six or so other preliminary English translations were all based upon the Traditional Text. And the same is true for virtually ALL other major translations of the Bible into other languages prior to the end of the 19th century. (The Latin Vulgate excepted.)

The text of the New Testament was never lost to history. It never has needed to be reconstructed. God has preserved His Word and in fact the very words of Scripture as Jesus said He would. It should not take a great deal of mental effort to notice which text has been the standard text in the first 18 centuries of Christian history. Prior to 1881, and with the basic exception of the Roman Catholic Vulgate,[20] the Traditional Text has been the text of Christianity.

We will now move on to the substantial issues which surround Codex Sinaiticus and Codex Vaticanus, the principal pillars of the modern Critical Text, whence virtually all modern translations derive. As we will see, they are neither oldest nor best.

Chapter Two – Neither Oldest Nor Best

End Notes:

1. There are also Old Testament textual differences between the traditional Ben Chayim Masoretic text used by the KJV and the more recent Hebrew text *Biblia Hebraica Stuttgartensia* used by most modern translations. However, for the purposes of this book, our focus will be upon the textual issue of the New Testament.

2. Kurt and Barbara Aland, *The Text of the New Testament*, translated by Erroll F. Rhodes (Eerdmans, Grand Rapids, MI, 1989), p. 26-30.

3.The term *eclectic* refers to a variety of diverse manuscript sources including elements of the Textus Receptus and textual fragments from other sources.

4. Over 1,000 additional Greek manuscripts of the Traditional Text type have been located in recent years at the Greek Orthodox Scriptoriums at Mount Athos which is near Thessalonika in Greece. The Greeks have not released these, but they have been made known by the Greek Orthodox Church. These are in additional to the approximately 6,000 manuscripts otherwise known to exist.

5. See *God's Perfect Book* by David Sorenson for further detail.

6. That philosophy is still the foundational principle which undergirds modern Critical Text editors.

7. Wikipedia: https://en.wikipedia.org/wiki/Codex_Vaticanus, 2016, 115-117.

8. The larger segment of Sinaiticus which Tischendorf "borrowed" did wind up in St. Petersburg, Russia. Later, when the Soviets were strapped for cash in 1933, they sold Sinaiticus to the British Museum for 100,000 pounds (worth about 6.4 million pounds in 2016 or more than eight million dollars).

9. John Burgon, *The Revision Revised*, Original publisher unknown, 1883. Reprint, Collinswood, N.J. Dean Burgon Society, n.d., p. 11.

10. Ibid., 319.

11. See *God's Perfect Book,* by David Sorenson, Northstar Ministries, 1820 W. Morgan St., Duluth, MN 55811, for further details.

12. Harvard educated Edward Hills explained how that Burkitt claimed the Peshitta was produced by one Rabbula, the bishop of Edessa, which was the capital city of Syria at that time. Burkitt therefore claimed that Rabbula's authorization of the Peshitta was somewhere between AD. 411 and 435. However, Burkitt's claim does not stand. There were two sects within the Syrian Church at that time and the Traditional Text was used by both sects. As Hills notes, "Since this division took place in Rabbula's time and since Rabbula was the leader of one of these sects, it is impossible to suppose that the Peshitta was his handiwork, for if it had been produced under his auspices, his opponents would never have adopted it as their received New Testament text" (172). Hills also quotes another historian who contends that Rabbula did not even use the Peshitta (174, n. 1). Hills continues, "If this is true and if Burkitt's contention is also true, namely, that the Syrian ecclesiastical leaders who lived before Rabbula also did not use the Peshitta, then why was it that the Peshitta was received by all the mutually opposing groups in the Syrian Church as their common, authoritative Bible? It must have been that the Peshitta was a very ancient version and that because it was so old the common people within the Syrian Church continued to be loyal to it regardless of the faction into which they came to be divided and the preferences of their leaders. It made little difference to them whether these leaders quoted the Peshitta or not. They persevered in their usage of it, and because of their steadfast devotion this old translation retained its place as the Received Text of the Syrian-speaking churches" (174). Edward Hills, Ph.D., *The King James Version Defended,* Des Moines, Christian Research Press, 1956, pp. 172-74.

13. Paul D. Yoonan, *History of the Peshitta*, 06/01/2000 http://www.peshitta.org/initial/peshitta.html.

14. For further details regarding the Peshitta and Italic translations, see David Sorenson, *Touch Not the Unclean Thing* (Northstar Ministries, Duluth, MN 2001), 78-81.

15. Frederick Nolan, *An Inquiry into the Integrity of the Greek Vulgate: or, Received Text of the New Testament* (London: F. C. & J. Rivington, 1815, 1815), xvii-xviii.

16. Harvard Theological Review 68 (1975), pp. 17-33.

17. Donald Waite, *Defending the King James Bible* (Collinswood, N. J., 1998) 47.

18. The New King James Version was fully published in 1982 and has received a modicum of success as far as modern Bible translations are concerned. However, though purporting to be based upon the Received Text, the NKJV in fact is literally peppered with marginal notes to the Critical Text (NU). And where there have been changes made in the NKJV in relation to the original KJV, the changes have largely followed the Critical Text. So much for it being based exclusively upon the Textus Receptus. It moreover uses the *Biblia Hebraica* Hebrew text for the Old Testament which is analogous to the Critical Text of the New Testament. In reality, the NKJV is thoroughly adulterated with critical readings in both the Old and New Testaments.

19. Adam Nicolson, *God's Secretaries: The Making of the King James Bible* (London: Harper Collins, 2005).

20. The Latin Vulgate Bible was the principal translation of the Roman Catholic Church from the time of Jerome in A.D. 382. However, what is not widely know is that Jerome did not work directly from Greek manuscripts, but rather his work was a revision of the *Vetus Latina*, which was a collection of biblical texts in old Latin. Though a number of vernacular translations of the Vulgate were produced during the time of the Reformation and onward, none of them nor the Vulgate itself has ever been given serious consideration by the vast majority of evangelical, Bible-believing Christianity.

Overview of the Issue

CHAPTER THREE

THE CHARACTER OF TISCHENDORF

In the drama about to unfold regarding the forging of Sinaiticus, a protagonist and antagonist will quickly emerge. That is, two principal characters will quickly take center stage and become bitter adversaries. A man by the name of Constantine Simonides will appear on the scene in Europe during the middle of the 19th century, making headlines in the European press and stirring great controversy. Simonides will very publicly claim that he produced Codex Sinaiticus in 1840. His antagonist will be a man by the name of Constantine von Tischendorf from Leipzig, Germany. Though initially colleagues, they will become bitter adversaries — and that very publicly.

As the story and evidence will unfold, you the reader will sit as a juror to determine the guilt or innocence of Simonides. He will be accused of being a liar and a fraud. A substantial part of the evidence will be the testimony of both Dr. Simonides and that of Dr. Tischendorf. As in a court of law, the attorney for the prosecution as well as that of the defense will seek to undermine the honesty and integrity of the opposition.

The Character of Tischendorf

As this author has read and sifted through many pages of history over the preceding months of preparation, I have felt like a juror hearing the opposing attorneys attack the credibility of a given witness. As I began this research, I honesty had an open mind. I, in fact, prayed and asked the Lord through His Spirit to lead me into all truth on this matter as per John 16:13.

The Lack of Integrity of Tischendorf

And so, let us first begin by looking more closely at the integrity and character (or lack thereof) of one of the principal witnesses in this case: Dr. Constantine von Tischendorf. Dr. Simonides was very publicly charged with lying about his claim that he was the producer of Sinaiticus. In a court of law, such a charge would be called perjury. The chief witness against him was Dr. Tischendorf.

Born Lobegott Friedrich Constantin Tischendorf (1815-1874), he was a gifted, educated, but ambitious Lutheran scholar. His mission in life was to publish a critical edition of the New Testament based upon what he considered to be the most ancient sources. His theological disposition was that the New Testament had been lost to antiquity. In his view, traditional-text-based Bibles such as Luther's German translation, and above all the King James Version in English, were corrupt and unreliable. Therefore, he set out to recover and restore the text of the New Testament through heretofore undiscovered ancient manuscripts. Though a "Christian" in a professional and nominal sense, there is no evidence whatsoever that the man was born again. He was essentially a German Rationalist. As far as he was concerned, the true New Testament had been lost to antiquity. He was to be the catalyst and hero in restoring it.

Moreover, as his discoveries piled up over a period of 20 or so years, he went from being an obscure research scholar to a highly celebrated and famous man about Europe. His discoveries brought not only honorary academic degrees, but literally fame and fortune. However, as we shall see, he was sorely lacking in integrity and honesty in pursuing his goals.

An opposing attorney might object that this background information is all irrelevant. However, we respond to the contrary. It all goes to help establish a motive for Tischendorf and his accusations against Simonides. This will be key in the coming controversies.

In May 1844, Mr. Tischendorf, when only 28 years old, made a journey to St. Catherine's Greek Orthodox Monastery located at the foot of Mount Sinai, in Egypt.[1] His purpose was to seek and discover ancient manuscripts of the New Testament. His account is:[2]

> "In visiting the library of the monastery, in the month of May, 1844, I perceived in the middle of the great hall a wide basket full of old parchments, and the librarian, who was a man of information, told me that two heaps of papers like these, mouldered by time, had been already committed to the flames. What was my surprise to find amid this heap of papers a considerable number of sheets of a copy of the Old Testament in Greek, which seemed to me to be the most ancient that I had ever seen."

What he had located were leaves (i.e., pages) of a manuscript which would come to be known as Codex Sinaiticus. The good doctor then went on to claim,

> "the authorities of the convent allowed me to possess myself of a third of these parchments, or about forty-three sheets, all the more readily as were destined for the fire. But I could not get them to yield up possession of the remainder. The too lively discussion I had displayed had aroused their suspicion as to the value of their manuscript."[3]

However, there are serious problems with this testimony. The evidence will show that Dr. Tischendorf was dishonest in his claim.

First of all, a brief discussion about the character of parchment is in order. Parchment is not paper. It is a flat, thin material made from the prepared skin of an animal and was used as a durable writing surface in ancient and medieval times. It is one of the several forerunners of the commodity of paper which we today take for granted in modern society. Whereas modern paper today is ubiquitous and cheap, parchment was neither. Animals such as a calf, lamb, or antelope had to be slain. It had to be skinned and then an extensive process of cleaning, stretching, and curing of the animal skin followed. A higher grade of parchment was called vellum. (In the testimony of this case, these two terms are sometimes used interchangeably. Though similar, they are slightly different.) The finished product then was cut into the rectangular shape resembling a large piece of paper. Scribes would then write thereon whatever the document at hand was about. Its purpose was very similar to paper, but its composition was not. It was a prepared animal skin.

The relevancy of this historical background to Tischendorf's claim is this. Paper readily burns. Parchment does not. Vellum (i.e., parchment) makes extremely poor kindling. It would be akin to using leather to kindle a fire. When put to flame, vellum will only smoulder and produce acrid smoke. Only a hot, established fire will cause it to readily burn.

Tischendorf clearly made up that story, perhaps unaware of the combustive characteristics of parchment or the lack thereof. Dr. Tischendorf committed perjury before the court of history. In so doing, he has shown himself dishonest and lacking credibility. The jury therefore should take notc of this misleading witness.

But there is more to this story. The monks of the Sinai monastery would no more be given to burning ancient manuscripts than anyone else would, even if the parchment would in fact easily burn. Stop and consider. Why would a librarian of a monastery renowned as a repository of ancient manuscripts use what purportedly was an ancient manuscript of Scripture as a source of kindling? The story is absurd on its face. A library is a place where ancient documents are treasured, protected, and stored; not burned.

Tischendorf claimed that the monks of the monastery allowed him to take with him one third of the manuscript ready to be burned which he in fact did. He brought it to the University of Leipzig library in Germany. It came to be known as *Codex Augustanus Frederico*, named after his patron — Frederick Augustus II of Savoy. This would be the genesis of many later honors and accolades for Tischendorf. Included were him being bestowed the German title of "von" which would be analogous to the English title of "Sir." It was an honorary title of nobility. He, moreover, was eventually granted an honorary Doctor of Divinity degree by a university in Germany and offered another by a university in Switzerland. He was also awarded several gold medals as his fame grew. Three foreign countries decorated him and one even caused a gold medal to be engraved expressly in recognition of his work. Discovering and producing Codex Sinaticus became a ticket to fame and fortune for Constantine Tischendorf.

What is particularly telling is that the descendants of the monks of the library at St. Catherine's to this day vehemently deny that permission was granted for Tischendorf to take forty-three leaves of a parchment. As will be soon established, the simple truth is that Dr. Tischendorf stole those forty-three parchment leaves of what would soon be known as Codex Sinaiticus.[4] And, as will be established in a coming section, those 43 leaves were found to be in exceptionally good condition for their purported antiquity.

But the plot continues to thicken. In 1853, Tischendorf returned to the monastery and tried to obtain the remaining leaves of the manuscript. He was rebuffed. He returned in January of 1859 under the patronage this time of Tsar Alexander II of Russia.

In 1859, Tischendorf again asked permission to take the codex to a sister monastery in Cairo where he would have assistance in copying the text. The sacristan Vitalios refused his request. He thence embarked on a course of duplicity which would continue for years to come.

Aware of the regional politics of the Greek Orthodox Church, Tischendorf played one faction against the other and was able to overrule the decision of the local sacristan at St. Catherine's. The higher ups of the Greek Orthodox Church in Cairo granted him permission to bring the volume to Cairo for the express purpose of copying it. Tischendorf now embarked even further with trickery which would continue for years to come.

With the assistance of two Germans, Tischendorf copied Codex Sinaiticus in two months, March and April of 1859. This amounted to 110,000 lines of text, plus 12,000 additional lines made by later editors.[5] He then departed from Cairo until the end of July whence he again sought to obtain the codex for the Tsar of Russia. He thus came up with a scheme wherein he informed the Greeks that the Tsar would support the cause of Cyril, a popular candidate for the office of archbishop, if the monks at St. Catherine's would give the codex to him altogether. They again refused. He then asked if he might *borrow* the codex in order to produce a facsimile edition at St. Petersburg, Russia. He told them he would have that project done by the fall of 1862, in time for the 1,000 year anniversary of the Russian monarchy.

What is of particular significance is that Tischendorf asked to *borrow* the manuscript. As history has recorded, he had no intention of ever returning Sinaiticus to St. Catherine's, and he did not. Once again the integrity or lack thereof of von Tischendorf may be observed. He was not a man of his word. Moreover, his actions belie him as a thief. He took Sinaiticus to Russia with the express assurance he was only borrowing it. But he never returned it.

The Character of Tischendorf

An inquiry was made in February 1861 at Mt. Sinai by the Rev. W. W. Wilcom of Salford, England, about a biblical manuscript sent thence by a German named Tischendorf to the Tsar of Russia. The librarian was confused about the matter and was unaware of any manuscript being given to the emperor. Mr. Wilcom was told that a manuscript had rather been loaned to the Russians. All attempts to identify a gift in connection with the name of Tischendorf were unsuccessful.

However, *The Literary Churchman* in 1862 wrote, "the account of Tischendorf was evidently made up." They asserted that Tischendorf lied about the whole affair. The monks from St. Catherine's monastery to this day argue that Tischendorf was lying. Interestingly, even today in the history of Sinaticus presented by the British library, they apparently believe that Tischendorf was lying because they do not mention most of what he said about discovering the first 43 leaves of the manuscript.

Even F. J. A. Hort of Westcott and Hort fame, in a letter to the editor of the British newspaper *The Guardian*, August 13, 1862, wrote, "parts of Tischendorf's language about his own discovery have been thought by some to leave room for suspicions." That is a remarkable admission from a man who largely built his fame upon the "discovery" of Tischendorf. To be sure, Hort believed Sinaiticus to be ancient. He only questioned Tischendorf's story about how he obtained it.

As it turned out, Tischendorf did in fact produce a printed edition of Codex Sinaiticus in the spring of 1862. The first copies were presented to the Tsar and Tsarina in October of that year. The original codex was then placed on exhibit at the Imperial Public Library in St. Petersburg, Russia. It was there entitled *Codex Sinaiticus Petropolitanus.*

The Russians evidently became aware of Tischendorf's chicanery with St. Catherine's Monastery in the Sinai. In 1869, they unilaterally proclaimed their possession of Sinaiticus to be a *donation,* though the monastery did receive 9,000 rubles from the Russian government. As history moved on, Russia became the Soviet Union. In 1933, Stalin's cash-strapped government sold Sinaiticus to the British Museum in London for 100,000 pounds where it remains to this day.[6]

Of course, this record is not universally accepted. Famed German textual critic Kurt Aland in 1993 delivered a public lecture endeavoring to defend Tischendorf and his acquisition of Sinaiticus. He based his defense of Tischendorf almost exclusively upon the discovery of letters which Tischendorf had sent to his wife from 1859-1869. In those letters, Tischendorf wrote to his wife the same story he told the world about his acquisition of Sinaiticus. It would seem rather that Tischendorf not only lied to the Greeks, but to his wife as well.

However, what prompted Aland to rise up in defense of his fellow German textual historian was an essay by a scholar named Ihor Sevcenko, entitled, *New Documents on Constantine Tischendorf and the Codex Sinaiticus.* In 1960, Sevcenko found several documents at St. Catherine's which contradicted the conventional wisdom of the Sinaiticus story as presented by Tischendorf. What Sevcenko found was a handwritten note written by Tischendorf himself promising to return the codex to St. Catherine's. In that note, Tischendorf wrote:

> "I the undersigned, Constantin von Tischendorf, now on mission to the Levant upon the command of Alexander, Autocrat of All the Russias, attest by these presents (sic) that the Holy Confraternity of Mount Sinai, in accordance with the letter of His Excellency [the Russian] Ambassador [to Turkey] Lobanov, has ***delivered to me as a loan*** an ancient manuscript of both Testaments, being the property of the aforesaid monastery and containing 346 folia and a small fragment. These I shall take with me to St. Petersburg in order that I may collate the original at the time of publication of the manuscript. (Italics and bold mine.)
>
> This manuscript has been entrusted to me under the condition stipulated in the aforementioned letter of Mr. Lobanov, dated September 10, 1859, Number 510. ***This manuscript I promise to return***, undamaged and in a good state of preservation, to the Holy Confraternity of Mount Sinai at its earliest request."[7] (Italics and bold mine.)

We again find damaging testimony as to the character and credibility of Dr. Tischendorf. He promised in a signed statement that his taking possession of Sinaiticus was a loan and he promised to return it. He clearly did not honor his word, He also undoubtedly knew the leadership of St. Catherine's had little or no leverage against him once he left Egypt, much less against the Tsar of Russia.

Sevcenko therefore asked, by what authority did Tischendorf offer Sinaiticus to the Tsar in 1862 especially if the Russians did not declare it a donation until 1869. What Sevcenko clearly implied is that Tischendorf was not forthright with the Tsar either. Sevcenko would observe that Tischendorf was a brilliant, erudite scholar, but also vain and devious.[8] Sevcenko would find another five documents at St. Catherine's which conclusively refuted any claim by Tischendorf that the monks there ever intended to donate Sinaiticus to the Tsar of Russia. Those documents also explained why ten years later in 1869 the Russian government finally made a token restitution and thus more or less legitimized their illegitimate possession.[9]

The record thus shows that Dr. Constantine von Tischendorf is not a credible witness. He has impeached his own character. This will come to the surface soon as the controversy with Constantine Simonides comes to light. It will be Tischendorf who will be the chief witness against Simonidcs. But Tischendorf had demonstrated to the world his lack of integrity.

But there is more. The story is long and complicated, but we will give the distilled essence. The ancient Greek mathematician and physicist Archimedes lived in the third century BC. He wrote among other things a document entitled "The Method of Mechanical Theorems." It showed up at the Greek Orthodox monastery of St. Savas near Jerusalem in the early 19th century and eventually to a library in Constantinople before 1844. To this day, it is considered extremely valuable. In fact it was sold for over $2,000,000 in 1998. But that ancient and valuable manuscript is lacking one leaf. Guess who had possession of the manuscript and absconded with the missing leaf? In 1845, Tischendorf presented documents to the Saxon Government from his recent trip in payment for their underwriting his travels. Included was this ancient manuscript without the missing leaf. After his death in 1874, Tischendorf's heirs sold the leaf along with other valuable documents to Cambridge University Library in 1876.[10]

The Character of Tischendorf

The Greek mathematician and historian Michael Lambrou is on record as saying that Tischendorf stole not only the missing page, but the entire document.[11]

It seems that Dr. Tischendorf came into possession of this page dishonestly. Though he was a brilliant scholar, he also quite clearly demonstrated himself as devious, a liar, and a thief. This impeachment of his character will certainly come to bear when considering his testimony against Constantine Simonides.

End Notes:

1. St. Catherine's Greek Orthodox Monastery was reputedly one of three locations for ancient biblical manuscripts in the Mediterranean world. Another was the Vatican. A third was several scriptoriums on Mount Athos in Greece, near Thessalonika.

2.Tischendorf: *When were our Gospels Written?* New York: American Tact Society, 150 Nassau Street, New York, 1867, pp. 23-24.

3. Ibid.

4. What Tischendorf brought from the Sinai was purportedly a fourth century uncial codex of the Septuagint version of the Old Testament. It contained part of I Chronicles and Jeremiah, and all of Nehemiah and Esther. He published those 43 leaves in 1846 as a facsimile edition.

5. What is significant about this time frame is that modern critics of Simonides attack his claim of copying Sinaiticus in less than 18 months, claiming that was not enough time to accomplish the task.

6. The British Museum's library department formally became the British Library in 1973. Sinaiticus is actually located at the British Library today.

7. Ihor Sevcenko, "New Documents on Constantine Tischendorf and the Codex Sinaiticus," *Scriptorium*, vol. 18 (1964) p. 61. Reprinted in the author's *Byzantine and the Slavs in Letters and Culture* (Cambridge, Massachusetts: Harvard Ukrainian Research Institute; Napoli: Istituto Unversitario Orientalie, 1991), p. 191.

8. Ibid., p. 80.

9. Dean Papademetriou and Andrew J. Sopko, *The Church and the Library: Studies in Honor of Rev. Dr. George C. Papademetriou,* 2005. Boston, Somerset Hall Press, 416 Commonwealth Avenue, Suite 117, Boston, Massachusetts, p. 86.

10. Ibid., p. 87-89.

11. Michael Lambrou, "Re: [HM] Archimedes Palimpsest," Internet message at http://sunsite.utk.edu/math_archives/,http/hypennail/historia/jul99/0034,html, 3.

The Character of Tischendorf

CHAPTER FOUR

THE CLAIMS OF SIMONIDES

A man in Europe arose to challenge Tischendorf and his claims about Sinaiticus. Needless to say, the fame and fortune of Tischendorf were at stake, not to mention the claim of antiquity for the manuscript of Scripture he had discovered.

That man was a Greek by the name of Constantine Simonides (1820-1867). Simonides openly disputed Tischendorf's claims about Sinaiticus. For almost four years Simonides very publicly argued that Sinaiticus was not an ancient manuscript, but that he himself had created it from 1839 to 1840.

Constantine Simonides was born on the Greek island of Symi in the Aegean Sea, near the coast of Greece. He grew up around the scriptoriums of the Greek Orthodox Church and his uncle was an official at the scriptorium of one of the monasteries at Mount Athos. Mount Athos is near the city of Thessalonika and is the home to 20 Greek Orthodox monasteries. For many centuries, these monasteries have been the literary hub of the Greek Orthodox Church. Most Byzantine copies of the New Testament were copied at Mount Athos over the centuries.

Simonides thus grew up in the heritage of many centuries of Greek scribes and Greek literature. It was second nature to him. Greek, whether the Koine Greek of the New Testament, classical Greek of ancient times, or modern Greek, was part of his upbringing. Accordingly, Simonides was a paleographer. Paleography is the study of ancient and historical handwriting (that is to say, of the forms and processes of writing). His uncle Benedict wrote, that Simonides "thoroughly acquired the art of paleography and became so great a proficient therein that few surpass him either in the practice of it, or in the diagnosis of manuscripts."[1]

Prior to the uproar which erupted after Simonides claimed that he himself had created Sinaiticus, he was highly regarded across Europe for his skills and knowledge of ancient literature. Simonides owned a collection of more than 5,000 ancient manuscripts, which he had partially inherited from his uncle. These manuscripts were presented at libraries and universities across Europe, often sparking academic debates. These debates usually revolved around the understanding of ancient languages. However, when Simonides publicly proclaimed himself the creator of Sinaiticus, attitudes changed, especially that of Tischendorf. James Farrer wrote in 1907, "That Simonides was a good enough calligrapher, even at an early age, to have written the Codex, is hardly open to doubt."[2] Though he maintained a modest and humble spirit, he considered himself to have superior knowledge of Greek literature over his European counterparts. He had grown up with it and they had not. At one point, even Tischendorf had spoken highly of Simonides.

Farrer further wrote, "His literary activity was extraordinary. Besides the works he published in Odessa, in England and in Germany, he wrote many others which were never published. His chief interest was to prove that his method of interpreting Egyptian hieroglyphics was superior to as well as different from that of Champollion and other Egyptologists." And, "In literary ability, he surpassed all his contemporaries."[3]

The controversy thus begins in Liverpool, England in 1860. There Simonides saw a copy of Tischendorf's facsimile of Codex Sinaiticus. He immediately recognized it and told others that he was in fact the calligrapher who created it. Simonides spoke of his authorship to J. E. Hodgkin in 1860.[4] He also wrote to Sir Thomas Philips on August 2, 1861 and mentioned the matter. British newspapers eventually picked up on the story and it was reported in 1861.

On July 27, 1861, *The Literary Gazette* printed,

> "We understand that in literary circles, a rumour prevails that the manuscript now publishing by the Russian government, under the direction of Mr. Tischendorf purporting to be a manuscript Bible of the fourth century, is not an ancient manuscript but is entirely a modern production, written by a gentleman now alive, who will shortly take measures to establish his claim to authorship. The manuscript is known as Codex Sinaiticus, and has attracted a large amount of attention through out Europe. Should the rumour prove to be correct, as we believe it will, the disclosures that will follow, must be of greatest interest to archaeology."

What particularly disturbed Simonides was that two renowned scholars proclaimed the codex to be authentic and of great age. Plymouth Brethren scholar Samuel Tregelles and Cambridge Professor Bishop

F.J.A. Hort sided with Tischendorf and against Simonides. Dr. Tregelles wrote a letter to the editor of the British newspaper *The Guardian* August 13, 1862, and said, "the story of Simonides . . . is as false and absurd as possible."

Simonides in turn wrote to *The Guardian* newspaper in September of 1862 and said,

> "When about two years ago, I first saw the facsimiles of Tischendorf, which were put into my hand in Liverpool by Mr. Newton, a friend of Dr. Tischendorf, I at once recognized my own work, as I told him immediately."

Simonides in turn replied to *The Guardian.* Below is the lengthy letter to the editor by Simonides and published in *The Guardian* September 3, 1862.[5]

THE SINAI MS. OF THE GREEK BIBLE

> Sir — As you have in your possession of August 13 a published letter from a correspondent signing himself F.J.A.H., in which reference is made to me, I must ask you for permission to make a statement in reply. Your correspondent favours you with some extracts from a letter written by Dr. Tregelles, in which the following sentence occurs:
>
> "I believe that I need hardly say that the story of Simonides, that he wrote the MS.,[6] is as false and absurd as possible."

The MS. referred to is that called the Codex Sinaiticus, now being published under the editorship of Professor Tischendorf, at the expense of the Russian Government. As what Dr. Tregelles calls my "story" has never been published, and as that gentleman can only have heard of it through an indirect medium, it may interest both Dr. Tregelles and your readers to have the "story" direct from myself. I will tell it as briefly as possible.

About the end of the year 1839, the venerable Benedict, my uncle, spiritual head of the Monastery of the Holy Martyr Panteleemon in Mount Athos, wished to present to the Emperor Nicholas I of Russia some gift which had from time to time been offered to the monastery of the martyr. Not possessing anything which he deemed acceptable, he consulted with the herald Procopius and the Russian monk Paul, and they decided upon a copy of the Old and New Testaments, written according to the ancient form, in capital letters, and on parchment. This together with the remains of the seven apostolic fathers — Barnabas, Hermas, Clement Bishop of Rome, Ignatius Polycarp, Papias, and Dionysius the Areopagite — they proposed should be bound in gold, and presented to the Emperor by a common friend.

Dionysius, the professional calligrapher of the monastery, was then begged to undertake the work, but he declined, saying that the task being exceedingly difficult, he would rather not do so. In consequence of this, I myself determined to begin the work, especially as my revered uncle seemed earnestly to wish it. Having then examined the principal copies of the Holy Scriptures preserved at Mount Athos, I began to practise the principles of calligraphy, and the learned Benedict taking a copy of the Moscow edition of both Testaments (published and presented to the Greeks by the illustrious brothers Zosimas), collated it with the ancient ones, and by this means cleared it of many errors, after which he gave it into my hands to transcribe.

Having then received both the Testaments, freed from errors (the old spelling, however, remaining unaltered), being short of parchment, I selected from the library of the monastery, with Benedict's permission, a very bulky volume, antiquely bound, and almost entirely blank, the parchment of which was remarkably clean, and beautifully finished.

First, I copied out the Old and New Testaments, then the Epistle of Barnabas, the first part of the pastoral writings of Hermas in capital letters (or uncial characters) in the style known in calligraphy as αμφιδεξιοσ (amphidexios). The transcription of the remaining Apostolic writings, however, I declined, because the supply of parchment ran short, and the severe loss which I sustained in the death of Benedict induced me to hand the work over at once to the bookbinders of the monastery, for the purpose of replacing the original covers, made of wood and covered with leather, which I had removed for convenience — and when he had done so, I took it into my possession.

Some time after this, having removed to Constantinople, I showed the work to the patriarchs Anthimus and Constantius, and communicated to them the reason of the transcription. Constantius took it, and having thoroughly examined it, urged me to present it to the library of Sinai, which I accordingly promised to do. Constantius had previously been Bishop of Sinai, and since his resignation of that office had again become Perpetual Bishop of that place.

Shortly after this, I was placed under the protection of the illustrious Countess Etleng and her brother, A.S. Stourtzas, by the cooperation of two patriarchs; but before departing for Odessa, I went over to the Island of Antigonus to visit Constantius, and to perform my promise of giving up the manuscript to the Library of Mount Sinai. The patriarch was, however, absent from home, and I, consequently, left the packet for him with a letter. On his return, he wrote me the following answer:

My dearly beloved Son in the Holy Spirit, Simonides; Grace be with you and peace from God.

I received with unfeigned satisfaction your truly valuable transcript of the Holy Scriptures — namely, the Old and New Testaments, together with the Epistle of St. Barnabas and the first part of the pastoral writings of Hermas, bound in one volume, which shall be placed in the library of Mount Sinai, according to your wish. But I exhort you earnestly (if ever by God's will you should return to the sacred Mount Athos) to finish the work as you originally designed it, and he will reward you. Be with me on the 3d of next month, that I may give you letters to the illustrious A.S. Stourtzas, to inform him of your talents and abilities, and to give you a few hints which may prove useful to the success of your plans. I sincerely trust that you were born for the honour of your country. Amen.

Constantius, late of Constantinople. — an earnest worshipper in Christ. Island of Antigonus, 13th Aug. 1841.

After I had received the above letter, I again went to visit the patriarch, who gave me the kindest and most paternal advice, with letters to Stourtzas after which I returned to Constantinople, and from thence went to Odessa in November, 1841.

In 1846 I again returned to Constantinople, when I at once went over to the Island of Antigonus to visit Constantius, and to place in his possession a large packet of MSS. He received me with the greatest kindness, and we conversed on many different subjects, amongst others, upon my transcript, when he informed me that he had sent it some time previously to Mount Sinai.

In 1852 I saw it there myself, and begged the librarian to inform me how the monastery had acquired it but he did not appear to know anything of the matter, and I, for my part, said nothing. However, I examined the MS. and found it much altered, having an older appearance than it ought to have. The dedication to the Emperor Nicholas, placed at the beginning of the book, had been removed. I then began my philological researches, for there were valuable MSS. in the library, which I wished to examine. Amongst them I found the pastoral writings of Hermas, the Holy Gospel according to St. Matthew, and the disputed Epistle of Aristeas to Philoctetes (all written on Egyptian papyrus of the first century) with others not unworthy of note. All this I communicated to Constantius, and afterwards to my spiritual father, Callistratus at Alexandria.

You have thus a short and clear account of the Codex Simonides, which Professor Tischendorf, when at Sinai, contrived, I know not how, to carry away; and, going to St. Petersburg, published his discovery there under the name Codex Sinaiticus. When, about two years ago, I saw the first facsimiles of Tischendorf, which were put into my hand at Liverpool, by Mr. Newton, a friend of Dr. Tregelles, I at once recognised my own work, as I immediately told him.

The above is a true statement of the origin and history of the famous Codex Sinaiticus, which Professor Tischendorf has foisted on the learned world as a MS. of the fourth century. I have now only one or two remarks to make. The name of the professional calligraphist to the monastery of St. Panteleemon was Dionysius. The name of the monk who was sent by the Patriarch Constantius to convey the volume from the Island of Antigonus to Sinai was Germanus. The volume, whilst in my possession, was seen by many persons, and it was perused with attention by the Hadji John Prodromos, son of Pappa Prodromos, who was a minister of the Greek Church in Tebizond. John Prodromos kept a coffee house in Galatas, Constantinople, and probably does so still. The note from the Patriarch Constantius, acknowledging the receipt of the MS., together with 25,000 piastres, sent to me by Constantius as a benediction, was brought to me by the deacon Hilarion. All the persons thus named are, I believe, still alive, and could bear witness to the truth of my statement.

Of the internal evidence of the MS. I shall not now speak. Any person learned in palaeography ought to be able to tell at once that it is a MS. of the present age. But I may just note that my uncle Benedict corrected the MS in many places, and as it was intended to be re-copied, he marked many letters which he purposed to have illuminated. The corrections in the handwriting of my uncle I can, of course, point out as also those of Dionysius the calligraphist. In various places I marked in the margin the initials of the different MSS from which I had taken certain passages and readings. These initials appear to have greatly bewildered Professor Tischendorf, who has invented several highly ingenious methods of accounting for them. Lastly, I declare my ability to point to two distinct pages in the MS, though I have not seen it for years, in which is contained the most unquestionable proof of its being my writing.

In making this statement. I know perfectly well the consequences I shall bring upon myself but I have so long been accustomed to calumny, that I have grown indifferent to it and I now solemnly declare that my only motive for publishing this letter is to advance the cause of truth, and protect sacred letters from imposition.

In conclusion, you must permit me to express my sincere regret that, whilst the many valuable remains of antiquity in my possession are frequently attributed to my own hands, the one poor work of my youth is set down by a gentleman who enjoys a great reputation for learning, as the earliest copy of the Sacred Scriptures.

The letter was repeated in *The Literary Churchman* 16th December, 1862, and *The Journal of Sacred Literature*, October 1862.

Subsequently after this letter, Simonides supplemented his story in another letter to *The Guardian* (January 21, 1863) in which he provided a further motive for copying the manuscript by hand.

> "The discovery of the library induced my uncle to establish a printing press at Athos for the dissemination of the various unpublished MSS and those which he was preparing for publication.
>
> For this purpose I was urged by him to go to Athens, and provide there everything requisite for printing. I went and placed myself under the direction of A. Coromela for a sufficient time, he being then the first printer in Athens, and on this account also some spoke disrespectfully of mc. I wrote to my uncle from Athens duly, that it was impossible for any one to obtain a proper printing press in Greece, because the Greeks themselves procured from France every requisite for printing. Being assured of this by others also, he recalled me to Athos. I sailed from the Piraeus in the month of November 1839, and landed again at Athos for the fifth time.
>
> After a few days I undertook the task of transcribing the Codex, the text of which, as I remarked before, had many years previously been prepared for another purpose. But Benedict, as well as the principals of the monastery, wishing to recognise with gratitude the munificence of the Emperor Nicholas on the one hand, and desiring on the other to acquire a printing press without expense, and being under otherwise to effect these purposes, decided that a transcript of the Sacred Scriptures should be made in the ancient style, and presented as a gift to the Emperor Nicholas, and he found that all the heads of the monastery perfectly agreed with him. Accordingly, having again revised the books ready for publication, the first Genesis, he gave it to me to transcribe.

A Summary of Simonides' Letters

Constantine Simonides was a Greek who could understand English, but was by no means fluent in it. His letter to the Guardian newspaper was in Greek and had to be translated into English. Thus, the letter at times does not flow as smoothly as one might expect. Moreover, the translation is in 19th century British syntax and spelling which is not always completely familiar to American readers in the 21st century. Furthermore, Simonides' initial letter is long, detailed, and complicated. The letter was originally written in long hand and it thus rambles. Therefore, let us present a reasonable summary of what Simonides wrote.

1. Simonides was asked by his uncle Benedict in 1839 to prepare a copy of the Bible, with several other apostolic writings in ancient (uncial) style of Greek writing as a gift to the Tsar of Russia. His uncle was one of the religious leaders of that particular monastery. This gift was (a) in gratitude for kindnesses the Tsar had shown to that particular monastery, and (b) it also was hoped the Tsar would provide funds for the monastery to purchase a printing press.

2. The staff calligrapher of the monastery, Dionysus, was leery of a project of such a magnitude and declined to take the lead on the project, though he would eventually assist Simonides. Benedict therefore asked his nephew Simonides to undertake the project. He agreed and began to practice the necessary calligraphy.

3. His uncle located and collated several Greek manuscripts principally the Moscow Edition and thus prepared a text for Simonides to copy. They determined to do so in uncial (upper case) letters which was the Greek style of writing in the early centuries of Christianity.

4. A codex (a volume of parchment) which was basically blank was found in the library of the monastery. Simonides removed the several pages already written upon and used the otherwise blank codex to copy out the Bible and several other early church writings (*The Epistle of Barnabas* and the *Shepherd of Hermas*).

5. He was assisted by the scribe Dionysus and his uncle in the project. The copying of the codex was completed in 1840 and done in relative haste resulting in many mistakes. His uncle Benedict therefore went back and made many corrections. (Other hands subsequently would also add corrections in the coming years.) Because of the many mistakes and corrections, the project was no longer thought worthy as a gift to the Tsar of Russia.

6. Rather it was determined to eventually send the book to the library at St. Catherine's Monastery at Mount Sinai.

7. However, other church leaders urged Simonides to redo the project such that it would be a suitable for a gift to the emperor of Russia. That was never accomplished.

8. Simonides directly accused Tischendorf of chicanery and fraud in claiming the antiquity of what came to be known as Sinaiticus.

In addition to being published by *The Guardian*, Simonides' letter was also published in the British newspaper *The Literary Churchman* on December 16, 1862 and in the *The Journal of Sacred Literature* in October of 1862. His claims were therefore widely publicized, particularly in England.

The Battle was Joined

For the next several years volley after volley was fired by Simonides defending himself on the one side and Tischendorf or his surrogates attacking him on the other side. The implication that Tischendorf had mistaken a manuscript of the nineteenth century for one of the fourth naturally roused Tischendorf to a condition of fury.[7]

In 1982, an entire book was written by J.K. Elliott entitled *Codex Sinaiticus and the Simonides Affair*. In it, Elliott produced in exhaustive detail the voluminous back and forth between Simonides, Tischendorf, and their surrogates. There were many letters to the editors and articles published either attacking Simonides or defending him. We cannot in this book begin to provide the virtually endless debate which erupted, almost entirely in England. Most of the material is sniping at details in Simonides account. When he would defend himself, then more nitpicking would erupt against him.

In reading through Elliott's book, one clear analogy became evident. The establishment press and academia, particularly of England, attacked Simonides much like the liberal press and the liberal political establishment in America will today attack a conservative candidate for political office. The left will stoop to whatever is necessary to defeat a conservative. Any possible detail will be harangued to destroy the conservative. And, it is no secret how vicious and biased the liberal media can be. While professing themselves to be nonpartisan, they have become cheer leaders for one particular political party and its liberal positions.

Such were the attacks upon Simonides. Any possible inconsistency, real or contrived, was trumpeted in the establishment press in excess to question, impeach, and destroy the integrity of Constantine Simonides. We will touch upon a little of it in the sections to come. But the most of it is not worthy of the space or time it would take to recount in this book. Suffice it to say, the liberal establishment of England did everything in its power to brand Simonides as a fraud and his claims as a hoax.

Many Details

In reading through Simonides' lengthy, rambling letters, one thing is apparent. It contains many details about people, places, and events. He mentions a specific place, the Monastery of the Holy Martyr Panteleemon at Mount Athos. He mentions a specific time, 1839, the end of that year to be more exact. He mentions specific individuals involved such as Benedict his uncle who though by then deceased, was known to many at Mount Athos. He mentions a calligrapher by the name of Dionysus the Areopagite. He mentions brothers by the name of Zosimas. He mentions specific source manuscripts such as the Moscow edition of both Testaments. He mentions a specific style of calligraphy such as amphidexios. He mentions a man by the name of Constantius who was of some note in Greek Orthodox circles. He mentions a man by the name of A.S. Stourtzas. He mentions a time line of events from his journey to the Island of Antigonus on August 13, 1841 to a trip to Odessa in November 1841, to a trip to Constantinople in 1846. He takes note of a journey to Mount Sinai where he once again saw his work there and commented how it had been altered to look old. He went on to mention other witnesses to his work such as Hadji John Prodomos. He even mentions where Prodomos worked at a coffee house in Galatas, Constantinople. He mentions another witness, the deacon Hilarion. And he mentioned an eyewitness to his work by the name of Kallinikos. He further mentioned pages in Sinaiticus which would bear distinct markings attesting to his writing of Sinaiticus.

That is an amazing list of specific details attesting to the veracity of his story. Those who prevaricate are usually not given to such specificity. Moreover, most of the men mentioned were still alive when all the controversy erupted in the early 1860s. *The Guardian* newspaper, which was very critical of Simonides, certainly had the resources, ability, and motive to send an investigative reporter to Greece to either verify once and for all or show that Simonides was a fraud. They did not. Of the specific individuals mentioned by Simonides such as Dinoysius the scribe, Germanus the Monk, Hilarion the deacon, or John Podromos the coffee-house keeper, none were ever sought out. They could have quickly confirmed or denied his account.

However, a surrogate of Tischendorf by the name of W. A. Wright did send a letter to the British Consul in Thessalonika, Greece, with a list of specific questions about Mount Athos and Simonides' account. A British Consul officer by the name of Richard Wilkinson replied to Mr. Wright and essentially said that the Simonides story was false.[8] Wright in turn passed that information on to *The Guardian* newspaper which published it on November 11, 1863.

However, those familiar with the local situation quickly countered Wilkinson's report. In the December 2, 1863 edition of the *The Literary Churchman* publication, J. E Hodgkin replied to Wright's charge. As it turned out Mr. Wilkinson of the British Consul did a very sloppy job of investigating. Of the numerous monasteries on and about Mount Athos, there were several rival sects. As is true in most religious groups, there are internal parties or subdivisions which often are at odds with each other and at times hostile to each other. Such was the case on Mount Athos. As previously mentioned, there were 20 Greek Orthodox monasteries of varying groups on or near Mount Athos. The two prominent orders were those of the *Coenoblac Order* and the other the *Idiorhythmic Order*.

Wilkinson contacted the head of the wrong group of monasteries. He contacted the head of the Xeropotami Monastery which was part of the *Idiorhythmic Order*. They were hostile and even bitter enemies to the *Coenoblac Order* to which Simonides was affiliated. Accordingly, they either did not have any pertinent answers for the consulate or even dissembled to Wilkinson about Simonides.[9]

In a coming section, a specific eyewitness would in fact come forth and defend Simonides and his work. He was either ignored by the establishment press or his credibility was attacked. Finally, the liberal establishment denied that he even existed. His name was Kallinikos. Much more will be said about him in a coming section.

By way of contrast, Tischendorf's version of events contained very few details and almost no names of individuals who might verify his story. It should be evident who was lying and who was telling the truth. Moreover, as described in the preceding chapter, Tischendorf was demonstrably devious, dishonest, and guilty of larceny.

In reading the letter from Simonides, the tone of his personality comes across as humble and almost naive in contrast to the pretensions of European elitist society. In distinction to Tischendorf's reputation as devious, Simonides was considered honorable and genuine by men such as Joseph Mayer of the Mayer Museum in Liverpool, the curator at the museum, J. E. Hodgekin, Charles Stewart, and others.

Stewart wrote a biography of Simonides defending him against a controversy that had erupted at the University of Leipzig with Tischendorf and another scholar named Dindorf in 1857. This happened several years before the procuring of Sinaiticus in 1859 by Tischendorf and then the subsequent conflict with Simonides thereafter. They thus had a knowledge of each other before hand. (In the incident in Germany, Simonides was charged with fraud by Tischendorf. He was arrested and brought before a German court. However, the court threw out the charges and exonerated Simonides. This will be dealt with in greater detail in a coming section.)

In that regard, Charles Stewart wrote, "I may add that the high opinion I entertain of Dr. Simonides as a gentleman and a man of honor at the time I published his biography has in no way diminished during the two years that have elapsed." He thus refers to the controversy in Germany. Stewart went on to say, "I know him to be utterly incapable of committing the disgraceful deeds imputed to him and firmly believe that the truth and value of his statements and discoveries will be universally admitted and recognized."[10]

In *The Dial* newspaper, published in London and dated January 17, 1862, a prominent scholar named Alexander von Humboldt was quoted regarding Simonides, "He is an enigma and that the mysteries and the injudicious commentaries upon him by which some have made themselves ridiculous arise from the imperturbable and naturally incommunicative character of Simonides." Though a bit obtuse in syntax, what Humboldt simply said was that the critics of Simonides had made themselves ridiculous. That is, their attacks against him were ridiculous.

What is almost astonishing is that before all the controversy between Sinaiticus and Tischendorf erupted, Tischendorf himself praised Simonides in February 1856. He said:

> "Simonides received an excellent education and when a young man spent a considerable amount of time in the Greek monastery at Mt. Athos occupying himself almost exclusively in the study of ancient manuscripts by means of which especially he greatly enriched his knowledge of the Greek and Egyptian antiquities. At the same time he employed himself very much in drawing and lithography in which he became very skillful and this skill was turned to account afterwards when he copied the ancient manuscripts.

> Moreover, by vigorous studying and voyages in Asia and Africa, Simonides arrived at the climax of superiority in philology, particularly in the knowledge of the wonderful art of ancient manuscripts."[11]

After publicly challenging Tischendorf's account regarding Sinaiticus, the debate erupted, particularly across literary and scholarly circles in England. Surrogates for Tischendorf such as W.A. Wright and Henry Bradshaw, curator of manuscripts at the Cambridge University Library, relentlessly attacked the credibility and integrity of Dr. Simonides.

Simonides continued to claim that the manuscript had not been created with any intention to deceive, but was intended all along, with his uncle, to be a gift to Tzar Nicolas I of Russia. To prove his claims, Simonides challenged Tischendorf to a public debate.

In January 28, 1863, *The Guardian* newspaper printed an open letter from Simonides to Tischendorf. In it he wrote,

> "Again I seriously assert (as Mr. Bradshaw seems to think I am jesting on this grave subject) that I wrote the Codex, to which Tischendorf has given the names of *Frederico-Augustanus* and Sinaiticus; *and I challenge him to produce these Codices in London.* I will meet him there at any time he may appoint, and in a public meeting of literary men assembled for the purpose it shall be once and for ever decided whether he or Simonides has spoken truly."

Tischendorf ignored the invitation to debate.

In turn, Simonides replied,

> "The real test of the genuineness of the Codex Sinaiticus is neglected. The public were (sic) assured in May, Tischendorf was to be in London, armed with a portion, at least of his great codex. I have waited in England, hoping to have the opportunity of meeting him face to face, to prove him in error, but May has come and gone, and the discoverer has not appeared. Let the favourers of the antiquity of the manuscript persuade him to come at once, and brave the ordeal, or else for ever hold his peace."[12]

It would appear that Tischendorf feared a public debate. Could it be that his claims for Sinaiticus would be exposed and his ticket for fame and fortune destroyed? He would not put his money where his mouth was.

One thing which Simonides had openly claimed was that he had placed several acrostics and monograms on the pages of Sinaiticus. These would confirm his account. Falconer Madan wrote in 1920, "Simonides asserted that not only had he written it, but that in view of the probable skepticism of scholars, he had placed certain private signs on particular leaves of the codex. When pressed to specify these marks, he gave a list of leaves on which were to be found his initials or other monograms. The test was a fair one, and the MS., which was at St. Petersburg, was carefully inspected. Every leaf designated by Simonides was found to be imperfect at the part where the mark was to have been found."[13]

Two important thoughts are at hand. (1) Tischendorf undoubtedly was aware of those identifying marks. And (2), when we get into the forensic evidence section of this book, we will verify that not only were those particular leaves in Sinaiticus "imperfect," but that they had been clipped or mutilated by human hands, quite apparently on purpose. There quite evidently was action taken by somebody, at some point to remove identifying marks from the manuscript by clipping the pages in question.

Paleography

At the nub of determining the date of Sinaiticus is an arcane discipline called paleography. One source says, paleography is the study of ancient and historical documents. Included in the discipline is the practice of deciphering, reading, and dating historical manuscripts, and the cultural context of writing, including the methods with which writing and books were produced.[14] As it pertains to the discussion at hand, it applied to determining the dating of a document. To this day, the principal means of dating Sinaiticus has been by paleography.

Notwithstanding the scholarly sounding name, paleography is actually very subjective. That is, a given paleographer determines the age of a given document pretty much by his own instincts. In the course of the ongoing controversy, Simonides directly asked Henry Bradshaw, the curator of manuscripts at the Library of the University of Cambridge, how he came up with the ancient date for Sinaiticus. Simonides also personally confronted Bradshaw about publicly defaming him.

Bradshaw wrote a letter to a friend about his encounter with Simonides. In it he stated,

> "Dr. Simonides wrote to me, to convince me and my friends that it is was quite possible for him to have written the volume in question. He had invited some of us to Christ's College to discuss matters fairly . . .. But the great question was, how do you satisfy yourselves of the genuineness of any manuscript? I first replied that it was really difficult to define, that it seemed to be more a kind of instinct than anything else. Dr. Simonides and his friend readily caught this as too much like a vague assertion and they naturally ridiculed any such idea. But I further said that I had lived for six years past in the constant, almost daily, habit of examining manuscripts."

Notice that Dr. Bradshaw based his conclusions regarding Sinaiticus upon "more of a kind of instinct than anything else."[15] That is highly subjective.

Consider this scenario. A paleographer/calligrapher determines to produce a counterfeit ancient document. (1) He obtains the necessary parchment. (2) Because he is learned in the ancient uncial style of Greek writing, he writes out the document in that style of lettering. (3) He then takes steps to make the parchment and ink look very old by scrubbing the document with an acidic liquid such as lemon juice mixed with special herbs. (4) He then washes the document with a solution of coffee or tea to give the parchment a slightly tan patina. (5) He then bakes the document in an oven to make the parchment leaves brittle and then roughens the edges of the pages. He then spills candle wax here and there and spills more coffee here and there — all to make the document seem old and tattered. He then binds the leaves of the document in a codex style of binding which also is dutifully processed to appear old.

Another paleographer comes along and examines the work. He notices that it is produced on what appears to be very old parchment. Moreover, it is written in the ancient uncial style of Greek lettering. The pages seem worn and to a certain degree brittle. In his professional opinion, he therefore comes to the conclusion that the document must date to the 4th or 5th century because that is when codex style of bindings had already begun to displace scroll type of documents. Moreover, the ancient uncial style of lettering lends credence to the antiquity of the document. The man who produced the document therefore sets a king's ransom for the price of the "ancient" document. The gullible buyer purchases it for the announced price enriching the unscrupulous calligrapher who produced the document.

Did such forgeries ever take place? They happened endlessly from the middle ages up through the nineteenth century. The Vatican, and especially the Jesuits, were expert at it. There are numerous verifiable forgeries produced by them over the centuries. Others less ideologically or theologically inclined did the same, but for ill-gotten gain. Even Tischendorf accepted a document as ancient in about 1855 in Leipzig, Germany, which was later thought to be of recent origin. More on this later.

The point is simple, however. Paleography as a means of dating is quite subjective and historically has been prone to many deceptions. In the case of Simonides, he made clear that he had no desire to deceive. However, he adamantly insisted that he had written Sinaiticus and that sometime after leaving his hands, it had been doctored to appear ancient in its appearance — at least the Codex

Sinaiticus Petropolitanus — the portion which he did not obtain until 1859 and which wound up in Russia.

In the mid 19th century, the only criterium for dating Sinaiticus to the 4th century were that (1) it was produced on parchment and not paper. (2) It was written in uncial style of lettering. (3) The pages and binding were the old codex type of binding. And (4) it certainly looked very old and tattered. That pretty much was how Tischendorf arrived at his dating of the manuscript. As for Tischendorf, it is the opinion of this author that he knew better, but claimed it was ancient nevertheless. In so doing, it certainly became a source of wealth and fame for him.

Simonides the Forger

In researching the life of Constantine Simonides, almost immediately the word *forger* or *hoaxer* will appear. A casual internet search will turn up such words in the article synopses on *Constantine Simonides.* And, again the name Tischendorf will appear for he was one of the first to accuse Simonides of forgery.

Simonides was not only a renowned paleographer of the mid 19th century, he also had a large collection of purportedly ancient manuscripts of varying topics ranging from history, to literature, to Scripture, to legal documents, and all of varying antiquity. He traveled across Europe visiting universities, museums, and libraries displaying his collection. He reportedly had in his possession over 5,000 manuscripts he was happy to display to scholars, the press, and anyone else interested in what he had. He was essentially a traveling museum of ancient manuscripts and documents. Much of this he had inherited from his uncle Benedict.

In 1855, Simonides appeared at the University of Leipzig in Germany. There he produced what appeared to be an ancient document entitled the *History of the Kings of Egypt: Up to the Reign of Ptolemy Lagus*. The author was a man by the name of Uranius of Alexandria, Egypt. It purportedly dated to the 12th century. That document came to be simply known as the Uranius Manuscript (or Uranius MS.).

Two professors at the University of Leipzig by the names of Dindorf and Anger accepted the manuscript as genuine but later changed their minds and claimed it was a forgery. Because they had paid Simonides 2,000 thalers, a considerable sum of money,[16] they reported the matter to the authorities. Simonides was summarily arrested and charged with fraud by way of forgery. He refunded his accusers on the spot. Whereupon he was transported to Berlin where he was acquitted of all charges. Inasmuch as the Uranius Manuscript was 10,000 pages in length (approximately ten times the length of Sinaiticus), that in itself mitigates against him forging it. It would take years to produce, no matter who did it. Nevertheless, two esteemed German paleographic professors thought the work genuine before changing their minds. However, the German courts did not deem the matter worthy of further prosecution.[17]

Unfortunately, Dr. Simonides thus came to be known as Simonides the forger. While in Liverpool, England, he was invited by the Mayer Museum of antiquities to examine several ancient papyri fragments. On display at Mayer's Museum were what purported to be a very old fragments of the Gospel of Matthew as well of I John 5:7. Joseph Mayer, the curator of the museum readily accepted them as authentic. Simonides claimed both fragments dated to the first century. These, of course, were astounding claims. If proven true, they would undercut the prevailing higher criticism of the New Testament. Whether they were that old or not is beside the point at hand.

Samuel Tregelles, an associate of Tischendorf, claimed they were forgeries by the hand of Simonides. However, the fragment of Matthew and I John had no connection to Simonides. Mayer obtained them years before he ever met Simonides. These historic fragments went on to be displayed at Cambridge University and then the Royal Museum of London. Critics continued to claim that Simonides had forged these and then sold them to Mayer as a fraudulent scheme. Yet, Mayer had purchased these documents from others years before he had ever met Constantine Simonides. But the moniker "forger" had been attached to Simonides. The establishment press would thereafter routinely refer to Constantine Simonides as Simonides the Forger. That epithet continues to this day.

In his original letter to *The Guardian* of September 3, 1862, Simonides wrote of knowing "calumny." The context was of his claim to writing Sinaiticus. He was speaking of being accustomed to being defamed as a forger and the accompanying derogatory comments about him. ***The poignant irony is that the one document he claims to have produced (Sinaiticus) was disclaimed, while he was routinely accused of having forged just about every other document he had ever touched. He openly said that he had produced Sinaiticus, but the establishment frantically denied it.***

In that context, Simonides sent another letter to *The Guardian* further protesting his defamation which was printed on January 21, 1863. He wrote,

> "Truly I wonder how people can credit such unreasonable falsehoods, things wholly impossible, and believe the reports of Tischendorf – viz., that I prepared palimpsests, and wrote 10,000 pages of an Egyptian Lexicon, 7,000 pages of the Alexandrine Philological Catalogue, 10,000 pages of Uranius! 8,800,000 pages of various other ancient writers on different subjects! That I corrected the corrupted texts of various classical writers, filled up many blanks of injured ancient MSS, and wrote and prepared papyri! And all this in a very limited space of time, for which work a life of two thousand years would not suffice me . . . ."[18]

Simonides thus pointed out how Tischendorf defamed him by claiming he had forged everything associated with him and the folly of that charge.

Another German 75 years later would advance the notion that "If you repeat a lie long enough, it becomes truth." That German was Joseph Goebbels. Though he did not originate that thought, he certainly believed it and practiced it. The same devious principle was applied to Simonides. The claim he was a forger has been told so often over the past 150 years that it is accepted as the truth in most circles even today.

In 1907 the book entitled, *Literary Forgeries* appeared written by James Anson Farrer.[19] Farrer presented an exhaustive list of documented forgeries of literature across the centuries. Included are such well known and documented forgeries as *The Decretals of*

Isadore, *The Donation of Constantine, The Decretum of Gratian*, the forged letters of Byron and Shelly, and many more.

What is of interest at this point is that Farrer included an entire chapter on Constantine Simonides with a section thereof about Sinaiticus. Farrer said of Simonides, "his industry, his learning, and his adventures claim for him a position apart, whilst it may be doubted whether any of his contemporaries in the learned world at all approached him in the art of calligraphy or in his knowledge of palaeography."[20] Farrer stopped short of accusing Simonides of "forging" Sinaiticus, mainly, I believe, from political pressures. But it is of interest nevertheless, that he included Simonides and Sinaiticus in a book about literary forgeries. The implication is that Farrer believed Simonides to have produced Sinaiticus without sticking his neck out and saying so directly.

Though Simonides to this day is routinely defamed as a forger, there has never been any definitive proof he forged anything. All that stands are the *allegations* of his enemies. The most vocal of these were those connected with the then developing Critical Text of the New Testament — the liberal establishment. Most of them were surrogates for Tischendorf. He had a vested interest in the antiquity of Sinaiticus for it was a principal part of his means to fame and fortune. His associates had a vested interest in defaming Simonides for if he were true, then one of the central pillars of the then developing Critical Text would be demolished. Moreover, their professional reputations would be made to look foolish. That same motivation continues to this day. The conventional critical-text establishment of the New Testament, both then and now, insist that Simonides be branded as "the forger." That club includes such names as F.J.A. Hort, Constantine Tischendorf, Samuel Tregelles, Henry Bradshaw, Bruce Metzger, J. K. Elliot, Kurt Aland, James White and others. Those contemporaneous with Simonides, virtually to a man, were associated in one way or another with Tischendorf.

An Eyewitness

The debate thus far was essentially the word of Tischendorf versus that of Simonides. Apart from the claims of each, another credible witness would emerge. His name was Kallinikos Hieromonachos. The latter word refers to his position or title within the Greek Orthodox Church — roughly rendered, a holy monk. He alternatively referred to himself as Kallinikos Hieromonk, or again, holy monk. As the debate raged, Simonides determined to call in reenforcements. His star witness was Kallinikos who gave testimony that he had personally witnessed Simonides producing the codex which would come to be called Sinaiticus. Moreover, Kallinikos would testify that he had witnessed Simonides discreetly place personal monograms and acrostics at several places in the codex, to verify his work.

Kallinikos Hieromonk

In *The Guardian* newspaper of December 3, 1862, and *The Literary Churchman* newspaper of December 16, 1862 two letters to the editors appeared with only minor differences from each other. They both were translated from Greek into British English and signed Kallinikos the Hieromonk. They are dated Alexandria, Egypt,

October 16, 1862, and bore the correct postmark from Egypt. The translation is below. The letter of *The Literary Churchman* is the basic letter as it is longer. The additions from the letter to *The Guardian* are in italics.[21]

> "You are aware of all that the excellent and much-enduring Simonides has published as to the Pseudo Sinaitic Codex, abstracted[22] from the library of the Greek monastery at Sinai, by Dr. Tischendorf. The facts are really so. And I counsel you not to continue circulating contrary statements, for you will greatly sin in foisting on the World a new MS as an old one, and especially a MS containing the Holy Scriptures. *Injury to the Church must accrue from all this, even from the evidently numerous corrections of the MS.* And that this is a new MS, I openly proclaim, both before the all-seeing God, and before men; and further, I protest to you, Messrs. Editors, that this is a genuine work of the indefatigable Simonides.
>
> For I myself saw him with my own eyes, in February, 1840, writing in the Athos; *and owing to the death of the head of the monastery, he left the work unfinished, and went to Constantinople, taking the Codex with him, which also he delivered to the illustrious patriarch Contantius, and he sent it to the monastery in Sinai by a monk of that house, named Germanus, whose subordinate still lives in Athos to attest the writer.* And the patriarch sent the Codex there, in order that the transcript might be compared with other copies of the Old and New Testament, and then he transcribed by the same Simonides, and sacredly presented to the Emperor of Russia, on the part, not of the monastery of St. Pantaleemon, *according to the original intention of*

Benedict, but on the part of the patriarch Constantius.

On this account, the hieromonk Callistratus, a wise man, *and companion of the same house*, undertook the comparison of it, and did compare it with other codices of the same house, by command of Constantius, the patriarch. And he, having partly corrected it, left it in the library awaiting the return of Simonides, *the first calligrapher in Greece*. He not coming in good time, the work was altogether neglected, and remained in the common library of the monastery for some time: until Dr. Tischendorf (coming to the monastery in Sinai, in May, 1844, and spending some days there, and having examined the MS carefully *and suspecting it to be ancient*), tore off a small part of it, privately, and went his way, as if nothing had happened, leaving the rest of it in the position which it had before. *He prepared this great wrong without scruple.* Finally, coming again to the same monastery, he took also the remaining portion of the MS with the aid of the Russian Consul, on the promise that he would return it. *And they both promised to the Bishop of Sinai many and great gifts, which, in my opinion, they will never perform: because, at other times, many such promises were made by a certain Russian archimandrite, named Porphyrius, who took away many MSS from the monastery of St. Dionysius, in Athos, and from others, and they were never fulfilled.*

All these things, then, I know being on the spot, and I declare them openly for the dear truth's sake. And I further assert, that the Codex which, *per fas et nefas*[23] Dr. Tischendorf abstracted, is the very same which Simonides wrote twenty-two years ago. For

> I saw it in the hands of Tischendorf, and recognised the work, and I first mentioned it to Simonides, who had no knowledge of the fact before.
>
> Evidently he knew not the abstraction of his work from the monastery in Mount Sinai. I read also at first this acrostic in it, "Simonides' entire work": but, after two days, the leaf containing this formal acrostic had been removed — it being unknown, as yet, by whom this was done. I know too, still further, that the same Codex was cleaned, with a solution of herbs, on the theory that the skins might be cleaned, *but in fact, that the writing might be changed, as it was, to a sort of yellow colour.*
>
> These things then, Messrs. Editors, I have thought it my duty, unasked, to make known to you before I die — for I am an old man, and very near to death; and you, being as you are, heralds of the truth — as such you will greatly serve the truth, and those who follow truth, if you will exactly publish the contents of this my letter; or, otherwise, you will give account to God in the Day of Judgment. Farewell in the Lord, &c."
>
> Your very devoted servant, and earnest
>
> Worshipper of God
>
> CALLINICUS HIEROMONK

As you the reader can attest, the letter from Kallinikos to the British press was verbose and rambling. Let me take the liberty to briefly summarize what Kallinikos said.

1. The letter had been sent from Alexandria, Egypt with proper post marking.

2. Kallinikos accused Tischendorf of having stolen the initial portion of Sinaiticus from the monastery at Sinai. (The British term *abstracted* is a euphemism for stolen.)

3. He further admonished these newspapers to stop publishing false statements; that is, Tischendorf's story.

4. He clearly stated that he personally witnessed Simonides producing the codex which would come to be known as Sinaiticus.

5. In the course of events, the unfinished project was sent to the Sinai monastery by a monk named Germanus.

6. Kallinikos again reiterated that he was "on the spot" as an eyewitness and also at Sinai when Tischendorf arrived in 1844 and absconded with a portion of the codex.

7. Kallinikos also noted that the personal identifying marks in the manuscript inserted by Simonides were removed while the codex was at Sinai. The portion of the manuscript which Tischendorf left behind had been washed with some sort of solution, leaving the pages thereof somewhat discolored.

Of interest is that on August 17, 1858, several years *before* all the uproar erupted, Kallinikos wrote a letter to Simonides from Smyrna, Turkey. In it are further details heretofore not revealed about the whole situation. In that letter, Kallinikos told Simonides that he had seen the manuscript, soon to be known as Sinaiticus when he had visited St. Catharine's Monastery in July of 1845.

Among other things, Kallinikos chided Simonides for having not carried through to completion what he had originally set out to do — prepare a gift for the Tsar of Russia. Below are excerpts of that letter.[24]

> "These also send thee greeting, the Deacon Hillarion, and thy friends Nicander and Niphon, who lent thee the Book of Esdras at the time when thou was preparing in Athos, at the exhortation of my uncle, the present (of the Holy Scriptures) to the glorious Emperor Nicholas.
>
> "They also wished to know whether the work was finished, and given to the Emperor, and whether thou wert suitably required for it: because they had no certain knowledge about these matters.
>
> "I told them all about it, and how thy indifference (forgive me, my son, for this true statement of mine) frustrated the original intention. I certified them that this MS. of the Scriptures is still preserved in Sinai (as thou also knowest), because I saw it there with my own eyes when I was in the Monastery of St. Catharine in 1845 in the month of July, and handled it with my own hands, and found it very defective, and somewhat changed."

Several comments bear making before proceeding.

1. This letter was written years before all the controversy erupted.

2. Notice that Kallinkos provided further specific details with specific names heretofore not mentioned: Nicander and Niphon.

3. Kallinikos was aware of the original purpose of producing a codex for the Russian emperor and saw it with his own eyes.

4. Moreover, Kallinikos made unflattering comments about Simonides, chiding him about indifference and essentially carelessness in not completing what he had originally promised to do: prepare a gift for the Tsar. He, moreover, told Simonides that others aware of the project wanted to know what had happened.

This is significant because very soon, the critics of Simonides would accuse him of making up the story of Kallinikos out of whole cloth. As the record shows, though a friend of Simonides, Kallinikos also accused him of being careless and indifferent. If Simonides had made up the story of Kallinikos, included were very embarrassing comments about him. Clearly, someone would not write and publish that about himself. (Bear in mind again that this was written several years *before* the controversy erupted.)

Kallinikos continued. Regarding his comment about the manuscript at Sinai having much changed since he had originally witnessed it at Athos when Simonides was producing it, he added:

> "When I asked the reason, I understood from Gabriel, the keeper of the treasures, that his predecessor had given the manuscript to a German, who visited the monastery in 1844 in the month of May, and who having had the MS. in his hands several days, secretly removed a part of it, and went away

> during the time that the librarian lay ill, afflicted with typhoid fever. Nothing more could I learn about it, but I hope (if God will) to go next year again into Egypt, and thence to Sinai, when I shall search into all things, and send the result for thy information and that of thy friends."
>
> Farewell, my son, and pardon the garrulity of an old man. Thy Spiritual Father,
>
> Kallinikos Hieromonachos

Again, let us make further comment about the remainder of Kallinikos' letter to Simonides in 1858. Again, recall that this is a translation into British English of a letter written in Greek.

1. Notice that additional detail is given in the name of Gabriel who evidently was the head librarian of the monastery.

2. He notes again how that Tischendorf, the German, had secreted away a portion of what would come to be called Sinaiticus.

3. Further detail is added in that Tischendorf was able to abscond with the first portion of the manuscript while the previous librarian at the time was sick in bed with typhoid fever.

4. Kallinikos refers to his garrulity, that is him being garrulous or verbose.

There in fact was a flurry of other letters back and forth between Kallinikos and Simonides, but that which is germane has been presented.

More Uproar

With the production of the letters of Kallinikos to the British press, an immediate campaign was launched to disavow Kallinikos. Several surrogates of Tischendorf, W.A. Wright in particular, like an adversarial attorney in legal proceedings, did everything he could think of to discredit Kallinikos and impeach his testimony. Wright was happily assisted by the editorial committee of *The Guardian* newspaper.

Wright tried to deny that Kallinikos had been in Alexandria, Egypt, when he said he was. He tried also to countermand details in the correspondence from Kallinikos. But Wright primarily claimed that Kallinkos and his uncle Benedict were figments of Simonides imagination and never existed. He claimed that Simonides had written the letters from Kallinikos himself. Wright further alleged that Simonides had then sent them to Alexandria, Egypt, and then had someone else re-post them back to England from Alexandria to carry the local postmark. Of course, there was no evidence that happened whatsoever. Nevertheless, these allegations against Simonides were all published in the British press as if they were fact. (And of course, here in America, we all know that the establishment media always gets the story right, particularly in regards to conservative type candidates or leaders.)

As noted earlier, correspondence was then made with the British Consulate in Thessalonika, Greece. A consular officer by the name of Richard Wilkinson was sent to Mount Athos to investigate Kallinikos and Simonides. However, as noted before, there were 20 monasteries on or near Mount Athos, not far from Thessalonika. Mr.

Wilkinson went to the wrong order of monasteries which denied they had ever heard of Simonides or Kallinikos. And of course, the false report of Mr. Wilkinson was trumpeted in the British press.

However, Kallinikos and Benedict did exist and there is documentary evidence that both of them and Simonides interacted at Mount Athos.

In the December 8, 1861 edition of the *Telegraph of Bosporus,* a Turkish newspaper, an Orthodox monk named Melchisedec of Laura, wrote, "That Benedict was distinguished both as a scholar and as a wise man, all those who knew his character admit."[25]

In 1895, Cambridge University published a two volume catalog of the contents of Mount Athos libraries compiled by a man named Spyridon Lambros.[26] Lambros was a Greek history professor at the University of Athens and was briefly the prime minister of Greece.

The Catalogue of Lambros made reference to Benedict in the 1840s. For example, there is recorded:

> "the teachings of Benedict according to Zoodohos Epidiorthopthi," catalogue number 5999; and, "various notes, additions, and miscellaneous teachings of Benedict" in catalogue number 6118.

There are four other specific entries in Lambros' catalog mentioning writings and entries belonging to Benedict in and about 1841.

There likewise are four specific references to Kallinikos in Lambros' *Catalogue of Greek Manuscripts on Mount Athos* from the 1840s to as late as 1867. For example,

> "by the hand of Kallinikos the ecclesiastical monk" (catalogue number 6389) and "By the hand of Kallinikos" (catalogue number 6406).

And there is another manuscript at Panteleemon, signed by Constantine Simonides on March 27,1841 (catalogue number 6405), and two other copies of the same work by Kallinikos Monachos (numbers 6406 and 6407), which prove that Kallinikos and Simonides were at Panteleemon at the same time and involved in the same work.[27]

There likewise are several entries referring to documents by the hand of Simonides at about the same time frame as Kallinikos.[28]

Lambros was no associate of Simonides. He was a renowned Greek historian who lived years after the fact. But he methodically cataloged the known documents and manuscripts located at the scriptoriums at Mount Athos and published his work in 1895. His work clearly authenticates the existence of Benedict, Kallinikos, and Simonides, all at the same relative time in history. The very title of his work, *Catalogue of Greek Manuscripts on Mount Athos*, connects Kallinikos, Benedict, and Simonides to the scriptoriums of Mount Athos in the mid 19th century. Moreover, Lambros use of καλλινικου μοναχου (Kallinikos the monk) is precisely how Kallinikos signed his letters to the British press.

Moreover, Kallinikos said that he had "lithographed at Moscow in 1853 and at Odessa in 1854 certain letters between himself and Simonides and the patriarch Constantius, wherein repeated allusion is made to the codex prepared by Simonides for the Tsar. One of these collections of lithographed letters is called "*Autographa*" and the other "*Spoudaion Hupomnema*." They are still both at the British Museum and were presented by Mr. James Young, an eminent antiquary, who received them as a gift from Simonides.[29] Moreover, these letters were written *before* the controversy erupted in1860-63.

Moreover, Mr. John Elliot Hodgkin set out in 1863 to try and get to the bottom of it all. He was informed by a "correspondent of unquestionable reputation at Odessa"[30] that the foreman of a lithography company in Odessa remembered the printing of the letters at the time claimed."

The charge that Simonides fabricated the story of Kallinikos is thus laid to rest. Historical data clearly has record of him at Mount Athos at about the time Simonides said he was. Furthermore, there are letters on record to this day between Simonides and Kallinikos, written *before* the controversy erupted discussing Simonides and his production of the codex which would become known as Sinaiticus.

Conclusion

The greater significance of all of this is that Simonides had an eyewitness who by his testimony corroborated the claims of Simonides. Though Tischendorf and his surrogates frantically tried to dismiss Kallinikos as they did Simonides, the record stands. Kallinikos was an eyewitness to the work of Simonides. "In the mouth of two or three witnesses, every word shall be established."[31] That should be the end of the story, but there is much more to come.

End Notes:

1. *The Dial*, August 2, October 4, 1861.

2. James Anson Farrer, *Literary Forgeries*. 1907. Bombay and Callcutta, Longmans, Green & Co., 1907, p. 59.

3. Ibid. P 65-66.

4. J. K. Elliott, *Codex Sinaiticus and the Simonides Affair*, Patriarchal Institute for Patristic Studies, Thessalonki, Greece, 1982. p. 26.

5. Ibid., pp. 27-31.

6. The standard abbreviation for an uncial manuscript is MS. The plural thereof is MSS.

7. Op Cit. Farrer, p. 59.

8. Ibid., pp. 71-72.

9. Ibid., p. 75.

10. Charles Stewart, *A Biographical Memoir of Constantine Simonides, Dr. ph., of Stageira, with a Brief Defence of the Authenticity of his Manuscripts*, C.J. Skeet, London, 1859, p. 78.

11. Chris Pinto, *Tares Among the Wheat*, Adullam Films, www.adullamfilms.com, 2012.

12. *Journal of Sacred Literature &Biblical Record*, Volume 3, 1863.

13. Falconer Madan, *Books in Manuscript*, 1920 (rev. ed.), London. p. 142.

14. Wikipedia definition of paleography.

15. Ironically, there is no evidence that Bradshaw or Tregelles ever saw the actual Sinaiticus manuscript, but rather only mechanically printed facsimiles thereof. There is no evidence that either of them traveled to St. Petersburg or Leipzig to view the actual documents.

16. A *thaler* was a Germanic silver coin used for almost 400 years in central Europe.

17. Elliot, op cit., pp. 123-128.

18. Ibid, cit. 26.

19. Op Cit. Farrer,

20. Ibid., p.39.

21. Ibid., p. 76.

22. The word *abstracted* is British usage and in this context is an euphemism for "stolen." Kallinikos will use the word or variations thereof several times and clearly believes that Tischendorf stole Sinaiticus from St. Catherine's Monastery.

23. The Latin phrase *per fas et nefas* translates roughly "whether right or wrong."

24. Op cit., Elliot pp. 86-87.

25. Ibid. p. 74.

26. Spyridon Paulou Lambros, Catalogue of the Greek Manuscripts on Mount Athos. 1895. (2 vols). Cambridge University Press.

27. Op cit. Farrer, p. 61.

28. Lambros cited by Bill Powers, *The Forging of Codex Sinaiticus,* Kindle edition, 2016, location 669.

29. Op cit. Farrer, p. 62.

30. Ibid. 63-64.

31. II Corinthians 13:1.

CHAPTER 5

THE FORENSIC EVIDENCE

Thus far, the story has revolved largely around the personalities of Simonides, Tischendorf, and their associates. Not much has been said about the actual document itself. But Tischendorf and Simonides aside, there is compelling forensic evidence to consider in the several portions of Sinaiticus located in Britain and Germany.

Let us briefly review the history of Codex Sinaiticus. In 1844 Tischendorf "discovered" the manuscript at the library of St. Catherine's Monastery at Mount Sinai in Egypt. He spirited away 43 leaves (86 pages) which he deposited in the library of his alma mater, the University of Leipzig in Germany. This portion of the original codex came to be known as *Codex Frederico-Augustanus* in honor of Tischendorf's patron at the time, King Frederick Augustus II of Saxony. The King in turn gave Tischendorf a gift of $5,000 which for the time was a princely sum. In 1846, Tischendorf published a transcribed facsimile edition thereof.[1] Moreover, the University of Leipzig created a professorship in his name in honor of his discovery and work.

In 1859, Tischendorf was able to once again, by hook or by crook, wrangle the remaining leaves from the monastery at Sinai. These in turn were taken to St. Petersburg, Russia, which at the time was the capital of Russia and the seat of new Tsar, Alexander II. Tischendorf named that portion of the original manuscript *Bibliorum Codex Sinaiticus Petropolitanus*, the latter word referring to St. Petersburg. As he did at Leipzig, Tischendorf then published a transcribed facsimile edition of Petropolitanus in 1862. The Tsar allowed Tischendorf to market the edition and keep all proceeds for himself, thus further enriching him.

But let us dig deeper into these two segments of Sinaiticus: *Frederico-Augustanus* and *Sinaiticus Petropolitanus*. The parchment leaves themselves have stories to tell.

Codex Frederico-Augustanus

As we shall soon see, the physical condition of the 43 Leipzig leaves were starkly different than the leaves which arrived at St. Petersburg, Russia. In 1856, a Russian scholar by the name of Porphyry Uspensky published a book entitled, *The First Trip to the Sinai Monastery in 1845.*[2] In it, Uspensky chronicled his research and journeys regarding Sinaiticus. Those travels took him also to Leipzig where he was allowed to examine Codex Frederico-Augustanus — the Leipzig segment of Sinaiticus. He had a most unusual and revealing comment to make about what he saw. He wrote that the leaves were of the "thinnest white parchment."[3] What is significant about this is that a manuscript

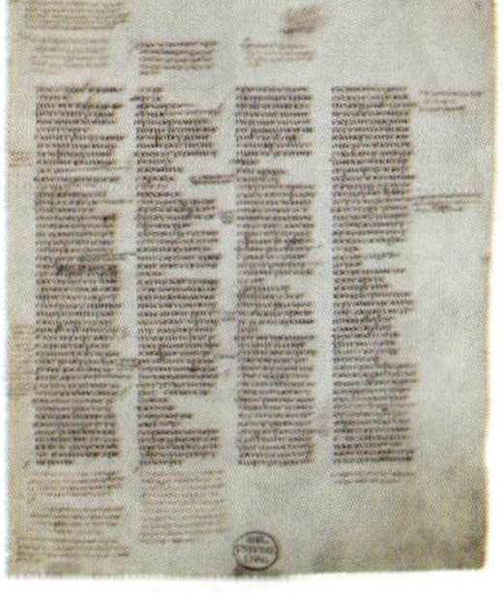

Codex Bezae
5th Century A.D.

Codex Sinaiticus
4th Century A.D. (Allegedly)

Codex Alexandrinus
5th century A.D.

Figure 1

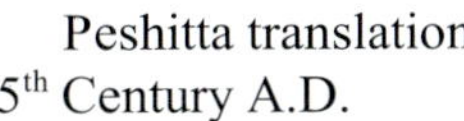

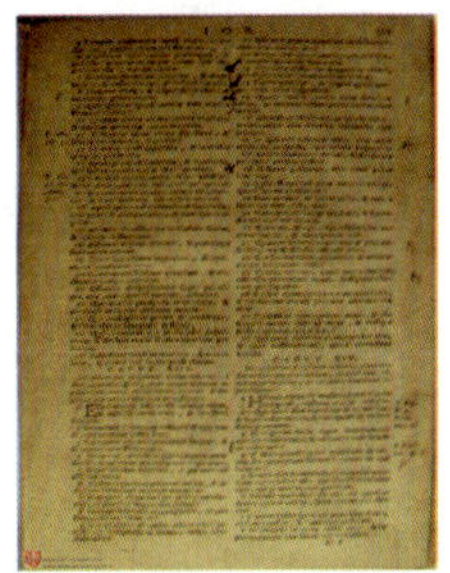

Peshitta translation
5th Century A.D.

Chester Beatty Papri
3rd century A.D.

Latin Vulgate
15th Century A.D.

Figure 2

Notice the coloration of each of the documents pictured above. With the exception of the page from Sinaiticus, all have a clear appearance of antiquity. Each of these digital photographs are taken directly from the British Library and have had no photo-shop editing done to them. There is no debate as to the antiquity of the age of the other documents.

Before the reader is prima facie evidence of the recent origin of Sinaiticus.

Figure 3

The reader will notice in the digital photograph of the leaf from Vaticanus above, where the Book of Hebrews begins, that there is an initial drop cap in the margin of the Greek letter "pi." This is the first letter of the Book of Hebrews. The artwork and initial drop cap are quite apparently medieval in character. The first word of Hebrews is "πολυμερως" (polumeros). After the initial drop cap, that word continues with the next letter "o," indicating the initial drop cap is integral to the text. This is typical for the entire manuscript of Codex Vaticanus. Most biblical books begin with an initial drop cap, integral to the text with artwork obviously medieval in character. See further discussion of this in chapter 7 and page 134.

document which is purportedly 1,500 years old will not contain *white* parchment. It rather will have parchment somewhere between a yellowed to brown complexion, but not pure white.

In 1910, German scholar Ernst von Dobschutz, also examined the leaves of the Leipzig portion of Sinaiticus. He commented about "the wonderfully fine *snow-white* parchment of the Sinaitic MS."[4] [Italics mine.] If there was any question as to the shade of white, Von Dobschutz left no doubt. There are few if any whites whiter than snow. Yet, that is the condition he saw. Once again, this is completely inconsistent for a document which is purported to be more than 1,500 years old.

In 1913, another scholar and eyewitness to Codex Frederico-Augustanus by the name of J. A. M'Clymont, wrote how that the manuscript leaves were "written on *snow-white* vellum."[5] [Italics mine.]

I have in my library an early edition of Spurgeon's *Treasury of David*, printed in 1872. The pages thereof are a shade of light tan. When a new sheet of laser-print copy paper, which might approximate being snow white in shade, is placed onto a page of one of those 1872 books, the contrast is stark. Those pages look dusky and old. Thus, parchment leaves which are 1,500 years old will not be snow white.

Codex Alexandrinus is another ancient manuscript of the Bible thought to have been produced in the fifth century. There really is no dispute as to its antiquity. However, in just the past several years, that manuscript has been made available online from the British Library through the precision of high-definition, digital color photography.[6] Its leaves are not snow white, but about what one might expect — dusky shades of tan that are almost brown. That makes sense for a manuscript which no one disputes is more than 1,500 years old.

We will discuss Codex Vaticanus in a coming chapter. But let it suffice to say at this juncture that pages of Vaticanus are not snow white either. Rather, they also are a dusky shade of coffee-tone, off-white. The same can be said of Codex Bezae, another ancient uncial codex dating to the fifth century. Very old manuscripts simply are not snow white in their appearance!

We have thus before us *prima facie* evidence for the relatively recent origin of the Leipzig portion of Sinaiticus. The parchment leaves thereof were snow white as late as 1913. In the mouths of two or three witnesses shall every word be established.

Please reference the illustrations in figures 1 and 2. In the digital photographs of figure 1, notice the coloration of Sinaiticus in the middle.[7] Then notice the coloration of codices Bezae and Alexandrinus on each side. They are profoundly different. Moreover, there is no dispute as to the dating of the Bezae or Alexandrinus. Before your eyes is *prima facie* evidence of the lack of antiquity of Sinaiticus. Furthermore, recall that Simonides noted that the coloration of the representative leaf picture above had been made to look older than what he had originally produced it. The leaves which went to St. Petersburg and eventually to London were artificially aged by parties unknown. The undoctored leaves at Leipzig were snow white in color.

In figure 2, notice the appearance of these additional ancient documents and their respective ages. They clearly have the appearance of antiquity. Even a 15th century copy of the Latin Vulgate is old and tired in appearance. Then notice again the photograph above of a leaf from Sinaiticus from the London collection. There is no apparent antiquity in its appearance. Apart from all the claims and counter claims of Tischendorf and Simonides, this is powerful and quite apparent evidence as to the relative age of Sinaiticus. It clearly is not ancient.

* * * * *

But the plot thickens. In 2009, the British Library in conjunction with the Leipzig University Library produced a high-quality, high-definition, digital-photographic facsimile of Codex Sinaiticus. A team of photographers visited the British Library, the University of Leipzig in Germany as well as Mount Sinai and St. Petersburg, Russia.[8] They used the same lighting and the same camera equipment at each location, endeavoring to maintain uniform conditions at each location. This was ultimately published by Hendrickson Publishers in 2011.[9] The volume is massive and very expensive, but it gives an exact, full-color reproduction of every page of the re-combined Codex Sinaiticus. One can essentially see the codex today which few earlier scholars and text editors ever saw.

Today, *all* the leaves (i.e., pages) of the manuscript are pretty much a uniform, dusky-white in appearance, including the Leipzig leaves

(Codex Frederico-Augustanus). Between 1913 and 2009, they went from snow white in appearance to a shade of off-white. Something happened in the intervening 96 years. They no longer look fresh and new. They look old in appearance. In those 96 years, they either quickly aged naturally from snow white to dirty white, or someone doctored them to give them the appearance of antiquity.

Codex Sinaiticus Petropolitanus

Recall how that Tischendorf managed to spirit away the first 43 leaves (86 pages) of his find at Sinai in 1844, and that he eventually was able to finagle the rest of it in 1859. However, small fragments of Genesis were left at Sinai. Also, another small fragment remained in Russia in 1933. These will be shown to have significance shortly.

Because the Russian portion was at St. Petersburg, recall that Tischendorf called it *Bibliorum Codex Sinaiticus Petropolitanus*. This is the portion of the manuscript which today is located at the British Library after the Soviets sold it to the British in 1933. However, the Petropolitanus portion of Sinaiticus has the appearance of some age. When Simonides saw the codex when he visited Mount Sinai in 1852, he complained that it had changed in appearance. He wrote, "The MS had been systematically tampered with, in order to give it an ancient appearance, as early as 1852, when, as I have already stated, it had an older appearance than it ought to have had."[10]

And, today, the entire manuscript, both the Leipzig and London portions, have a uniform appearance of age. They both are dusky shades of off-white. When Tischendorf absconded with the final portion thereof in 1859, it looked older. And, it does to this day.

Bill Cooper in his book *The Forging of Sinaiticus*[11] quotes Arthur Lucas, author of a most interesting work called *Forensic Chemistry*.

> "Occasionally documents are discoloured intentionally in order to give them a fictitious appearance of age . . .. Discoloration due to age is largely a process of oxidation brought about by natural means and it takes place in proportion to the extent to which the paper has been exposed to the air and light, and hence the outsides and edges of old documents, which are the most exposed, become the most discoloured, the discoloration progressively diminishing towards the less exposed parts."[12]

Lucas continues,

> "Artificial discoloration made to simulate age is produced by means of a coloured solution. The author has never been able definitely to establish the nature of any solution employed, but in the East coffee is very probable, while in the West tea might be used. A water extract of tobacco or a dilute solution of potassium permanganate would also serve the same purpose. The use of a coloured solution is generally indicated by the characteristic shape of the edges of the discoloured areas, or the way in which the liquid has run may be plainly visible, and a thin dark line sometimes occurs where there were any very marked creases on the paper at the time it was treated. Occasionally too portions of the paper, often very small, may be found which have altogether escaped the action of the solution."

And so, the question arises, is there any evidence that Codex Sinaiticus has been artificially discolored to give the appearance of age? The answer to that is an absolute yes. In examining the Hendrickson digital color facsimile, there are clear signs of tampering.

Uniform Coloration

As forensic chemist Arthur Lucas noted above, natural aging of document pages starts from the outer edges. Those areas of the manuscript or codex will be oxidized more than the interior. However, in perusing the current condition of Sinaiticus, the pages are pretty much uniform in their basic coloration from their edges to the interior of each page. That is an indication of artificial coloration.

Scrubbing

A technique used by literary forgers was to scrub a piece of parchment with an abrasive substance, perhaps with the aide of a light acid such as lemon juice. The result was that the ink of the text was dimmed and became a bit fuzzy, aiding in giving a forged document the appearance of age.

Is there evidence of textual scrubbing in Sinaiticus? Indeed, there is. Ironically, it is not consistent. Some leaves (pages) have columns of crisp and clear text. Then, a few pages over will be washed out. In some cases, the worker evidently was careless in his work and one can readily see where the scrubbing was done carefully and halfway down the page it was done carelessly. In fact on more than one occasion, on a given page, the upper portion of it has been scrubbed while the lower half of the page has not. It is quite apparent if one looks for it. Many examples could be cited. An examination of Sinaiticus will reveal some pages of crisp, clean text only to be followed by pages which are dim and fuzzy — all in the same volume and often within the same quire of the same biblical book. Once again, the scrubbing work quite apparently was done in haste.

Streaking

Another technique used by forgers was to stain the pages of a manuscript to give it the appearance of age. Consider staining a piece of wood. The stain is usually applied to a piece of cloth or even poured onto the work piece. The rag then spreads the stain across the surface. If it is done in haste or carelessly, there will be *streaks* across the surface which are not uniform. Some areas will be lighter and some will be darker.

Are there telltale streaks across the pages of Sinaiticus? Indeed, there are. In *many* places the coloration of the leaves (pages) are streaked. It is quite apparent if one looks for it.

Consider staining a piece of wood again. If the worker is particularly careless or perhaps is called away from his project after having applied the first swipe of stain, there will be a very noticeable dark streak of the stain across the work piece.

Did such carelessness appear in Sinaiticus? Yes, it did. One leaf (page) has a very ugly streak of stain which was never wiped out. It is clear someone was trying to discolor the leaf but for whatever reason did not finish his work on that page.[13]

The evidence is compelling. Throughout the codex, a staining agent was rubbed over the leaves, but it is uneven in many places. There clearly are veins of coloration across pages where either more or less stain was applied, but not carefully rubbed to an even consistency. The work evidently was done in haste.

Suppleness of the Parchment

On a manuscript purportedly 1,650 years old, the parchment will tend to be stiff and brittle, in addition to discoloring of the leaves, and fading of the text itself. Such is the case of Codex Alexandrinus which is dated to the 5th century. However, the parchment leaves of Sinaiticus are amazingly supple.

Since Tischendorf brought the manuscript portions back to Europe, the British Library in particular has done analysis of it. On their website describing the "Sinaiticus project" they state:

> "Although skin materials are remarkably durable given reasonable conditions of storage, collagen fibres nevertheless degenerate slowly especially when exposed to water vapour, light and heat. Fluctuations in humidity and excessive moisture levels can result in hydrolysis which, in the presence of natural and man-made pollutants such

> as sulphur dioxide or nitrogen dioxide in the atmosphere, can catalyse oxidisation. This process of deterioration leads initially to a reduction in strength of the dermal fibre network causing phenomena such as curling and shrinkage. Over a prolonged period it can lead to a complete breakdown of the fibre structure and more permanent damage such as brittleness, splits and losses . . .. *The conservation team discovered that, despite being over 1,600 years old, the pages of Codex Sinaiticus held at the British Library consisted of a supple, high quality parchment in relatively good condition....* Much of the visual parchment evidence cannot answer many of the questions asked by those seeking proof about the origins of the Codex and the story of its survival."[14] (Italics mine.)

To summarize, the experts at the British Library were surprised by how fresh and supple the parchment was. In fact, they candidly admit that the physical evidence of the manuscript does not fit the claim of its antiquity.

A week before Hendrickson Publishers released their digital color facsimile of Sinaiticus, the British Broadcasting Company released a YouTube video of a news item (February 7, 2011).[15] In the video, a curator of the British Library casually flips pages of the codex as he gives a brief history and analysis. What is striking is how supple the leaves are. He seemingly has no concern of them being brittle. To the contrary, they indeed are still quite supple. That is *prima facie* evidence of the relatively recent origins of the manuscript. If it actually were 1,650 years old as claimed, its pages would be brittle and the curator would have handled it far more carefully.

The physical evidence of the parchment itself does not fit the claims of ancient origins. It all points to a document which is not old, but of relatively recent production.

Worm Holes

Because parchment is an animal skin and thus a type of flesh, it is an attractive food source for some insects and worms. Are there worm holes in the leaves of Sinaiticus? Yes, indeed. But what is particularly damning evidence are several worms holes where the scribe wrote around them.[16] There certainly are other holes in the leaves and they go right through the text on both sides. That is to be expected. But for the writer to work around the holes clearly indicates that the leaves of the parchment had been in existence for a while before he began his work. Recall how that Simonides said that he took a basically blank codex from the library at the St. Panteleemon Monastery at Mount Athos. The worm holes, with text going around them rather than the other way around, is powerful evidence that the manuscript was produced as Simonides said it was. Some worm holes already existed in the parchment leaves and Simonides just wrote around them.

Another curious fact is that the worm holes in the codex are singular. That is, on a given page, there might be a worm hole, but there is no evidence of it on the pages before or after. The worm or insect which made the hole clearly did not do so while the book was closed. The only possible way such holes could happen is when the leaves were out of the binding of the volume and exposed. Once again, that fits Simonides' story of how he unbound the blank codex at Mount

Athos and then wrote out each page separately. While in that unbound state, worms or insects had a meal overnight.[17]

Mutilation by Human Hands

Some of the amazing occurrences in Sinaiticus are several places where there is clear indication of physical alteration done by human hands. It is one thing when age, decay, worms, or rodents damaged the leaves. But it is another when human hands have literally cut out portions of pages.

On the leaf which should contain Number 6,[18] most of the page has been cut out. There is a rectangular section of the page missing, with a right angle cut near the bottom of the page. Morever, it appears that the edge of that cut was burned by a candle and then the burn snuffed out, giving a ragged, darkened edge. What is significant is that the portion removed is a rectangular, right-angle cutout. No rodent, worm, or decay would make such a pronounced rectangular cutout.

On the leaf where I Chronicles 17[19] should be, all that remains is a rectangular fragment which would approximate about ten percent of the page. The edges of this fragment have not been otherwise marred and it appears that the fragment was cut out of the page with a shears or scissors. Once again, no rodent, insect, worm, or any other natural cause is possible. Somebody took a shears or scissors and cut out a section of the page.

A similar incision is found on the leaf where the passage of the apocryphal book Judith 11:19 is. It is larger in size than the one in I Chronicles, but it is a very clear rectangular excision of most of that page.

What is most remarkable are several leaves where all appearances are that someone took a straight edge and then pulled a pen knife along the edge to make a perfectly straight cut, removing a section of the page. One such example is the leaf on which the book of Philemon appears. A very clear vertical cut is evident where about a half of the page has been excised. It clearly has been cut with the use of a straight edge. There is also a similar horizontal excision of another page which clearly was done with the aide of a straight edge.

Now, what is one to make of this quite obvious human intervention in excising portions of several pages throughout the manuscript? The answer may be quite simple. Recall what Simonides announced that he had done. One historian wrote,

> "Simonides asserted that not only had he written it, but that in view of the probable skepticism of scholars, he had placed certain private signs on particular leaves of the codex. When pressed to specify these marks, he gave a list of leaves on which were to be found his initials or other monogram."[20]

Moreover, the same historian also wrote,

> "the MS., which was at St. Petersburg, was carefully inspected. Every leaf designated by Simonides was found to be imperfect at the part where the mark was to have been found."[21]

In addition, when Simonides challenged Tischendorf to bring the manuscript to a public debate so that he could publicly display the pages with his monograms or initials, recall that Tischendorf refused.

The answer seems apparent. Either Professor Tischendorf or agents working on his behalf removed portions of those pages or otherwise mutilated them so that Simonides' identifying marks could not be found. The first such clumsy attempt was in the biblical book of Numbers wherein the one mutilating the text tried to burn the edges of the cut to make them seem irregular and jagged. Thereafter, perhaps as time became an issue, the mutilator simply took a shears or penknife and straight edge and removed the identifying evidence.

Also of interest is when Tischendorf absconded from Sinai with the initial 43 leaves segment, he left behind several leaves from early in the book of Genesis. Could it be, there was one or more identifying marks on them? And of further coincidence, the several leaves which were left at St. Petersburg, also were the initial pages of Petropolitanus. Could it be they also had incriminating markings on them?

One thing is for sure. Human hands cut out portions of a number of pages. It is more than just coincidence that *all* of the pages on which Simonides claimed he had left identifying marks were either missing or had sections thereof cut out. Tischendorf had access of the basic manuscript or had control over it at its several locations: Leipzig, St. Petersburg, and Sinai. May the jury reach a decision on the issue.

Carbon 14 Dating?

In doing research for this chapter, this author has had ongoing email correspondence with the British Library. For the most part, they have been helpful and answered questions promptly. However, there is one question they did not answer. I asked them if any other means of dating Sinaiticus had been utilized other than paleography. Recall that the original dating was based upon the *opinion* of Dr. Tischendorf, Mr. Bradshaw, curator of the curator of manuscripts at the Cambridge University Library, and that of Dr. Samuel Tregelles, a Plymouth Brethren scholar. In their *opinion*, Sinaiticus was produced in the fourth century, around A.D. 350. Ironically, there is no evidence that Bradshaw or Tregelles ever personally saw the actual manuscript, but only mechanically-printed facsimiles thereof. It really came down only to the *opinion* of Tischendorf himself.

Knowing that, I pressed the curator if more objective dating methods such as radio carbon 14 dating had been utilized to approximate the date of the manuscript.[22] Though carbon 14 dating is not a reliable tool for accurate dating, it can give a ballpark number. It, for example, could give some sense whether Sinaiticus is 170 years old or 1,700 years old.

The curator of ancient western manuscripts at the British Library never answered my inquiry, though prior thereto, he had been quite cordial. Officials of the British Library surely must be aware that there are substantial questions about the antiquity of Sinaiticus. In fact, there presently is as much discussion and debate on the question in Britain as in the United States.

The fact they would not reply to this question, when they had answered other inquiries, is revealing. There are several possible reasons. (1) They have not taken the pains to subject a tiny portion of the parchment leaves for carbon 14 testing and are embarrassed to admit that. Or, (2) they have in fact done so and the results do not support an old age of the manuscript. To be sure, carbon 14 dating involves destroying a small portion of parchment material to accomplish the test. But in light of the controversy which has gone on for at least 150 years, one would think they would attempt some sort of empirical, objective dating method. And, there are sections of margins and other blank areas which would not impugn the text in any way.

The silence of the British Library at this point is deafening. They could put to rest once and for all the burgeoning evidence that Sinaiticus is only 175 years old. Or, maybe they know that is the case and are not saying. Let the jury reach its own conclusion.

End Notes:

1. It should be noted that facsimile editions of the 19th century were not digitized photographic reproductions such as are available today. Rather, the original document was hand copied into Greek characters (transcribed) and then mechanically printed. Hence, the reader only saw the transcribed version of the original document and none of the peculiar characteristics of it.

2. Porphyry Uspensky, *The First Trip to the Sinai Monastery in 1845*. 1856, St. Petersburg, Russia.

3. Ibid. p. 226.

4. Ernst von Dobschutz, *Hastings Encyclopaedia of Religion and Ethics*. 1910. New York, Vol. 2., p. 583.

5. J. A. M'Clymont, *New Testament Criticism: Its History and Results*. 1913. Hodder & Stoughton, London, p. 44.

6.http://www.bl.uk/manuscripts/Viewer.aspx?ref=royal_ms_1_d_viii_fs001r

7. The reader should note that the author/publisher has not in any way altered the appearance of these photographs, but has taken them directly and without modification from the official websites of the British Library.

8. Though the principal portions of Sinaiticus are located at London and Leipzig, several small fragments of Genesis 21:26-22,17 and 23:19-46 were discovered at Mount Sinai in 1975. Another small fragment of Genesis 23-24 evidently remained in Russian hands when they sold the rest to the British Library in 1933. It continues today at the National Library of Russia. However, the vast majority of Sinaiticus today is at the British Library and a lesser amount at the Leipzig University Library.

9. *Codex Sinaiticus: Facsimile Greek Edition*, 2011. Hendrickson Publishers, Peabody, Massachusetts, ISBN 159856577X.

10. J. K. Elliott, *Codex Sinaiticus and the Simonides Affair*, Patriarchal Institute for Patristic Studies, Thessalonki, Greece, 1982. p. 26. *The Guardian* newspaper, September 3, 1862. Cited by Elliott.

11. Bill Powers, *The Forging of Codex Sinaiticus,* Kindle edition, 2016

12. Arthur Lucas. *Forensic Chemistry*. E. Arnold & Company, London, 1921. p. 79.

13. Q83-f.6r which is I Corinthians 16.

14. http://www.codexsinaiticus/en/project/conservation_parchment.aspx

15. https://www.youtube.com/watch?v=U4Xkv2gjzZw

16. Q88-f.7r which is Acts 25.

17. When this author was a pastor in central Florida years ago, he one day noticed a rather large cockroach literally munching on an old Young's Analytical Concordance in my library. It had been working on the book overnight and when I arrived in the office in the morning, I interrupted his illicit meal. The ugly bug was making a meal of the binding of the book.

18. Q11-f.2v

19. Q29-f.7r

20. Falconer Madan, *Books in Manuscript*, 1920 (rev. ed.), London. p. 142.

21. Ibid.

22. This author is well aware of the shortcomings of carbon 14 dating. It tends to be unreliable and is useful only under the best circumstances for only several thousands of years.

CHAPTER SIX
INTERNAL EVIDENCES

As the evidence has been presented, we have considered the direct claims of the personalities involved. We have considered forensic, physical evidence of the manuscript. Let us now look at another area of evidence — internal textual issues. Though this chapter will delve into literary history and technicalities of Greek and Latin literature, both ancient and modern, it is not necessary for the reader to know Greek or Latin. We will endeavor to set forth the evidence in such a way that just about anyone can understand it. Appendices are available with technical detail.

The Shepherd of Hermas

Recall that Codex Sinaiticus was a compilation in Greek of not only the New Testament, but the Old Testament, and some apocryphal books. Two of the latter from early church history were also included in the volume. One was the *Shepherd of Hermas* (sometimes called the Pastor of Hermas). The other was the *Epistle of Barnabas*. These both would prove to be: (1) an embarrassment to Tischendorf, and (2) potent evidence against the ancient dating of Sinaiticus.

The *Shepherd of Hermas* is an apocryphal Christian literary work thought to have been written either at the end of the first or mid-second century. It was comprised of sermons and parables which paid special attention in calling God's people to repentance. It drew upon the motif of the Good Shepherd in Scripture. The book was originally written at Rome in Greek, but a Latin translation, the Vulgata, was made very shortly afterwards. A second Latin translation, the Palatine, was produced at the beginning of the fifth century.[1]

A copy of the *Shepherd of Hermas*, as noted above, was an integral part of Sinaiticus, included at the end of the volume. It was thus of the same age and provenance of the greater codex. It was written on the same vellum parchment, with the same ink as the rest of volume, and by the same scribe. However, the salient point is that it was written in what is essentially modern Greek (medieval to 19th century) and not ancient classical or Koine Greek. That is the point of this chapter.

The Story Behind the Story

In 1855 Simonides arrived at the University of Leipzig, before all the controversy and rancor surrounding the dating of Sinaiticus had erupted. Among other things, he produced a copy of the *Shepherd of Hermas* written in Greek. What is significant is to that point in history, the only copies of Hermas to exist were written in Latin. Since Hermas had originally been written in Greek, the scholars at Leipzig were ecstatic with the prospects of what appeared to be an ancient copy thereof. Two professors of the University by the names of Dr. Wilhelm Dindorf and Dr. Rudolf Anger therefore had the work published. The literary world was astonished that at last a copy of the ancient Hermas in Greek was available. It was given the pretentious name *Codex Lipsiensis* — the Leipzig Codex.

Meanwhile, Professor Tischendorf familiarized himself with the recent discovery. To the consternation of Dindorf and Anger, Tischendorf pronounced the manuscript to be a fake — the work of a forger. He did not accuse Simonides of the forgery. He assumed he also had been deceived by it. But Tischendorf announced that the copy at hand was not ancient Greek, but rather a re-translation back into Greek from a medieval Latin edition. It was not ancient, but of relatively recent origin. In this area, Tischendorf indeed was expert, having translated the Latin Vulgate Bible into Greek. He accordingly was knowledgeable and adept in spotting Latinisms in both vocabulary and grammar.

In short, Tischendorf reported that the copy of Hermas — Codex Lipsiensis — was full of vocabulary and grammatical constructions which were typical of modern Latin and not of ancient Greek.

Whoever had translated Hermas back into Greek was familiar with modern Latin and not of ancient Greek. An analogy might be someone writing a document purportedly to be from Shakespearian England, but full of modern American slang and culture. The vocabulary would immediately betray the piece as modern in its origins. Similar was the copy of Hermas at Leipzig.[2]

So what does all of this have to do with the dating of Sinaiticus?

First, the copy of Hermas included in Codex Sinaiticus was of the same binding, the same parchment, the same ink, the same scribe, and the same provenance. That in itself is instructive. But the copy of Hermas at the back of Sinaiticus was virtually identical to that of Codex Lipsiensis — the copy of Hermas at Leipzig, now declared to be a forgery. And Simonides himself had said that he had copied out the Shepherd of Hermas into what came to be known as Sinaiticus.

* * * * *

Meanwhile, several years passed by and the very public debate over Sinaiticus had erupted. Tischendorf was in a quandary. By now he had published all of Sinaiticus. The copy of Hermas in Sinaiticus was virtually identical to the forged copy. It was part and parcel of the Sinaiticus manuscript. He thus faced this dilemma.[3] If he continued to claim that the copy of Hermas at Leipzig was a forgery, then it would be apparent that Sinaiticus also was.

Tischendorf's Flip Flop

If his declaration that Codex Lipsiensis was correct and that it was of relatively recent origin, then Sinaiticus was also of recent origin. The grammar and vocabulary of Lipsiensis proclaimed it to be not of ancient Greek. Tischendorf was forced to admit that his original declaration about Lipsiensis was wrong. He backpedaled and announced he had made a mistake and that Lipsiensis rather really was in fact based upon an ancient Greek text. If he had not, then it would be evident that Sinaiticus was also of recent origin. To protect his greater interest of being the one who had discovered Sinaiticus and its purported antiquity, he flip flopped his opinion. Ironically, Tischendorf's retraction of Hermas being a forgery was printed in Latin in an obscure German literary work which was hardly noticed by the general public or would have understood it in any event.[4]

Sir James Donaldson

But that is not the end of the story. In 1874, a British scholar by the name of James Donaldson released a book entitled *The Apostolical Fathers: A Critical Account of their Genuine Writings and of their Doctrines*. In it, he directly contradicted Tischendorf's flip flop and, with irrefutable evidence, proved that the copy of the *Shepherd of Hermas* included in Sinaiticus was in fact of recent origin. The year 1874 ironically was the year that Tischendorf died.

Donaldson was no literary lightweight. In fact, he was one of the great literary experts on ancient literature in the world at the end of the 19th century. His resumé and list of literary achievements dwarfed that of others of his day, including Tischendorf.

He had been elected a Fellow of the Royal Society of Scotland. In 1881 he became Professor of Humanity at Aberdeen University, and in 1890 Principal of St Andrews. In addition to his earned doctorate, he was awarded two honorary doctorates by Glasgow and Aberdeen Universities. He was the author of: *A Modern Greek Grammar for the Use of Classical Students*, 1853; *Lyra Graeca, Specimens of Greek Lyric Poetry from Callinus to Alexandros Soutsos*, 1854; A *Critical History of Christian Literature and Christian Doctrine from the Death of the Apostles to the Nicene Council*, issued in three volumes between 1864-1866; He collaborated on the writing and editing of *The Ante-Nicene Christian Library*, published in twenty-four volumes between 1867–72; *The Apostolical Fathers*, of 1874, in which he offered his analysis of the Shepherd of Hermas; *Lectures on the History of Education in Prussia and England*, also in 1874; *Expiatory and Substitutory Sacrifices of the Greeks*, 1875; *The Westminster Confession of Faith and the Thirty-Nine Articles of the Church of England*, 1905; and finally, *Woman, her Position and Influence in Ancient Greece and Rome*, published in 1907. Additionally, he wrote books in German and Latin, and many pamphlets, articles, lectures, talks and debates in which he was engaged in over the years. He further merited two biographical entries, one in the *New International Encyclopedia*, published in New York in 1905, and another in the *Encyclopedia Britannica* of 1911. For his literary achievements, King Edward VII of England conferred knighthood upon him in 1907.[5]

James Donaldson was thus an authority with few peers. Regarding the copy of Hermas within Sinaiticus, he wrote,

> "The late origin of the Greek text [of the Codex Sinaiticus Hermas] is indicated by the occurrence of a great number of words unknown to the classical period, but common in later or modern Greek . . .. The lateness of the Greek appears also in late forms . . . and some modern Greek forms . . . have been corrected by the writer of the manuscript . . . But if we consider that the portion which has now been examined is small, and that every page [of the Sinaiticus Hermas] is filled with these peculiarities, the only conclusion to which we can come is, that

> the Greek is not the Greek of the at least first five centuries of the Christian era. There is no document written within that period which has half so many neo-Hellenic forms, taken page by page, as this Greek of the Pastor of Hermas."[6]

To briefly further summarize his scholarly statement, Donaldson said in effect that many words in the text of the copy of Hermas in Sinaiticus were unknown in ancient times and are rather of later or modern Greek. He further noted that *every* page has these more modern words. It is not the Greek of the fourth century. In fact, no document from ancient times had these words found in the *Shepherd of Hermas* included in Sinaiticus. He confirmed Tischendorf's original assessment before he flip flopped.

Donaldson continued referring to Greek words translated from modern *Latin* found in the Hermas copy of Sinaiticus.

> "The peculiarities which point out a Latin origin are the following: There are, first, a number of Latin words where you would naturally expect Greek . . .. Then there is a considerable number of passages [of the Hermas] preserved to us in Greek by Origen and other writers. The Sinaitic Greek (Codex Sinaiticus) differs often from this Greek, and agrees with the Latin translation, especially the Palatine. There is every, especially internal, probability that the Greek of the ancient writers is nearer the original than the Sinaitic."[7]

His point is simple. There are a considerable number of places in the copy of Hermas of Sinaiticus where the Greek words are based on later Latin derivation. These do not agree or comport with ancient versions of Hermas such as existing copies written by Origen.

Rather, the Sinaiticus Greek version of Hermas agrees with later Latin versions and not ancient Greek. It was recent and not ancient.

In short, Donaldson demonstrated that the copy of Hermas contained in Sinaiticus is not from the fourth century, but of relatively recent origin. Recall again that the Hermas section of Sinaiticus is an integral part of the whole. It was bound in the same original volume. The leaves are the same. The ink is the same. The scribe is the same. In short, the rest of Sinaiticus was copied at the same time as the Hermas section. This is proof positive that Sinaiticus is not ancient in its origin.

For a full statement of Donaldson's technical appraisal of Sinaiticus and Hermas, see Appendix A.

The Epistle of Barnabas

Another apocryphal book found in Sinaiticus is *the Epistle of Barnabas*. It too has similar grammatical and vocabularic anomalies as found in Hermas.

The *Epistle of Barnabas* is another apocryphal book which was written in Greek either at the end of the first century or early in the second. It is not the same as the *Gospel of Barnabas*. It is not canonical — that is, it is not inspired. Some ascribe it to the Barnabas mentioned in the book of Acts, while others attribute it to some other unknown early Christian teacher. The latter is more likely. Though the work is not totally Gnostic, it has hints thereof. The main point of the epistle is a distinction between the church and

Israel and that the gentile church is now the true covenant people of God. Jews no longer are a part of God's covenant promises. Though right in pointing out that the entire Jewish sacrificial and ceremonial system have been abolished in favor of "the new law of our Lord Jesus Christ,"[8] the epistle erred in promoting what essentially was an early form of replacement theology. The latter is that the church has replaced Israel in God's plan and covenant.

Like the Shepherd of Hermas, the *Epistle of Barnabas* was part and parcel of the volume of Sinaiticus. It was an integral part of the codex as were all the other various books, canonical or otherwise. Like Hermas, Barnabas contains modern Greek words that were not used in ancient, classical Greek. It likewise is amply sprinkled with modern Latinisms — that is, words and phrase unique to Latin, indicating this particular copy of Barnabas had been translated from a later Latin translation.

James Donaldson thus critiqued Barnabas as he had Hermas. The essence of his appraisal is that Barnabas was translated into modern Greek from recent Latin. He thus concluded that the copy of *the Epistle of Barnabas* found in Sinaiticus was of recent origin and not ancient in its writing. When considering that both Hermas and Barnabas were integral parts of Sinaiticus — the same parchment type, the same ink, the same scribe, and the same provenance — the inescapable conclusion is that Sinaiticus is not ancient but of recent origin. That is exactly what Simonides had repeatedly asserted.

The full technical critique of *The Epistle of Barnabas* by James Donaldson of 1874 is found in Appendix B of this volume.

Donaldson, of course, was immediately pilloried and attacked for his audacity in questioning what by then was the conventional wisdom — the antiquity of Sinaiticus. Scurrilous articles appeared in several British newspapers savaging his ability and credibility. One anonymous review of Donaldson's work in *The Saturday Review* dismissed him as probably a layman.[9] Such an unlearned remark only revealed the ignorance of the writer of the stature of Donaldson. Recall, that the King of England would later bestow knighthood on him for his literary accomplishments. But his academic stature and reputation remains. Though the establishment press and their acolytes attacked him much like the modern liberal media will attack a conservative candidate, their volleys just bounced off. Moreover, the critics of Donaldson, vociferous as they were, were never supported. His basic charge regarding Hermas, Barnabas, and Sinaiticus remain. Donaldson challenged the antiquity of Sinaiticus through his analysis of Hermas and Barnabas. That analysis once again demonstrated their usage of modern vocabulary and grammar not found in ancient classical Greek. That assessment remains to this day — unchallenged.

However, the story gets even more interesting. On July 22, 1843, Simonides published a Greek edition of *The Epistle of Barnabas* at Smyrna in Turkey. What is significant is that the text of this published edition is virtually identical to the copy of Barnabas contained in Sinaiticus.[10] What is of further significance is that this was 16 years *before* Tischendorf finagled the final portion of Sinaiticus from St. Catherine's, when he departed in 1859.

Thus, if Simonides had possession of a manuscript of Barnabas to the degree that he published it in 1843, and if the copy of Barnabas included in Sinaiticus had the same vocabularic and grammatical anomalies of Simonides' edition, it follows that Simonides must have copied it into Sinaiticus, and by extension the entire codex. That in itself is further clear evidence that Sinaiticus was produced around 1840 by Simonides.

But the story continues. Later in July 1843, a Greek newspaper by the name of *The Star of the Sea* published a congratulatory article about how Simonides had recently published *The Epistle of Barnabas* at Smyrna. This is independent verification that Simonides published Barnabas in 1843 as he said.[11]

But the critics of Simonides would not give up. In 1876, after Donaldson had published his damning book undermining the antiquity of Sinaiticus, another British newspaper called the *Athenaeum* wrote a lengthy article in which it alleged that (a) Simonides had at a later date, presumably in the 1860s, published his edition of Barnabas and had placed the date of 1843 on the title page to make it look like it was published in 1843. (b) They further alleged that there was no newspaper called *The Star of the Sea* in Smyrna. And, (c), Simonides had gone to the trouble of faking the copy of that newspaper and dating it to 1843.[12]

However, the article in the *Athenaeum* was completely wrong. *The Star of the Sea* newspaper did exist and archival copies of are still in existence.[13] How foolish to allege that Simonides would forge an entire book to place a false date of 1843 on its title page and to fake a newspaper just to put a date of 1843 on its masthead. It shows how desperate the establishment was to preserve the claim for antiquity of Sinaiticus. But history is sometimes stranger than fiction.

Like the episode of Hermas, the lesson of Barnabas only served to further verify that Sinaiticus is of relatively recent origin. Though Donaldson did not come right out and say that Simonides was right, his research did it for him. The evidence is powerful and remains uncontradicted.

End Notes:

1. https://en.wikipedia.org/wiki/The_Shepherd_of_Hermas

2. Bill Cooper, *The Forging of Sinaiticus* Kindle edition, 2016, location 767.

3. Albrecht Dressel, *Patrum Apostolicorum Opera*, Leipzig, J. C. Hinrichs - Bibliopola1863, pp. xxxix-lv.

4. Ibid.

5. Cooper, op cit., location 811.

6. James Donaldson, *The Apostolical Fathers: A critical Account of their Genuine Writings and of their Doctrines*, MacMillan and Co., London, 1874, pp. 389-390.

7. Ibid., p. 390.

8. https://en.wikipedia.org/wiki/Epistle_of_Barnabas

9. *The Saturday Review*, January 2, 1875, p. 22-23.

10. Cooper, op cit., location 967.

11. Σιμονιδεσ, Κωνσταντινος. Η πρους τους εξ Εβραινων πιστους επιστολη αποστολικου πατρος ημων Βαρναβα. 1843. Σμυρνα [Smyrna]. (Roughly translated: Simonides, Constantine. The production on parchment of the faithful apostolic letter of our Father Barnabas, 1843, Smyrna.)

12. *The Athenaeum*. 8th January 1876, pp. 53-54.

13. Cooper, op cit., location 2518.

CHAPTER SEVEN

THE ISSUES OF VATICANUS

The reader will recall that the modern critical text, whence virtually all modern Bible versions derive is based principally upon two manuscripts: Codex Sinaiticus and Codex Vaticanus. These two comprise the vast majority of the modern critical text. Hence, the credibility of modern Bible versions rests upon the integrity of these two manuscripts. As we have already seen, Sinaiticus has somewhere between little and no integrity as an ancient manuscript. The evidence all points to its production in the 19th century. As we begin to consider Vaticanus and the issues connected to it, we will find there will likewise be major questions about its integrity and even its antiquity.

As we have examined the history of Codex Sinaiticus, it has been a story of intrigue, conspiracy, of charges and countercharges. The principal characters were flamboyant and controversial. The history of Codex Vaticanus surely is not as colorful. But there are serious issues which bear upon both its integrity and antiquity.

Dean Burgon's Assessment

In the mid 19th century when the famous liberal textual editors, Westcott and Hort, were developing what would become the modern critical text, there was a conservative textual scholar in England by the name of John Burgon. As a Dean in the Church of England, he was one of the preeminent textual scholars of his day. He quickly would become the nemesis and arch rival of Drs. Westcott and Hort. Whereas in private, Westcott and Hort were archetypical theological liberals, questioning the most basic tenets of biblical Christianity, Burgon was a rock-ribbed conservative. He was on record as saying:

> "I believe that the Bible is the Word of God — and I believe that God's Word must be absolutely infallible. I shall therefore believe the Bible to be absolutely infallible."[1]

Burgon continued,

> "But if . . . I am asked whether I believe the *words* of the Bible to be inspired, — I answer, to be sure I do, — everyone of them; and every syllable likewise."[2]

He also wrote regarding the scriptural writers,

> "they neither spoke nor wrote one word of their own: but uttered syllable by syllable as the Spirit put it into their mouths." [3]

Contrast the forceful declarations of Burgon with the questioning and doubting of inspiration by Westcott and Hort. The difference is as day and night.

In 1860 Burgon was permitted to view Codex Vaticanus at the Vatican for an hour and a half and was allowed to consult only 16 different passages.[4] In his considered view, codices Sinaiticus, Vaticanus, and Bezae were the most corrupt biblical documents in existence. It was his assessment that each of these codices, including Vaticanus, clearly exhibited a fabricated text and were the result of arbitrary and reckless revising.[5] As we proceed to examine Codex Vaticanus, we shall see that Burgon's assessment was true.

The Conventional History of Vaticanus

The conventional wisdom of the history of Vaticanus is that it was produced early in the fourth century at Alexandria, Egypt. It may have been one of 50 Bibles commissioned by Constantine the Great for the churches of Constantinople in the 4th century.[6] Internal textual characteristics lend itself to Egypt in the fourth century.[7] Some have thought that the codex may have been housed in a library of Caesarea in the sixth century A.D., though this all is only speculation.

But the first *concrete* historical record of Vaticanus is in A.D. 1475 when it appeared in the catalogue of the Vatican Library. There is *no* specific historical record of the manuscript prior thereto. From thence to this day, its shelf number (library reference number) at the Vatican Library is 1209.

When Desiderius Erasmus was preparing his third printed edition of the Greek New Testament in 1521, he corresponded with Paulus Bombasius, Prefect (i.e., head librarian) of the Vatican Library. Erasmus enquired regarding what is known as the Johannine

Comma, that is whether I John 5:7 was found in Vaticanus.[8] It was not (and is not). The greater point at this juncture is: this is the first record of anyone consulting Vaticanus for any research. There is no record of it being used for anything prior to 1521.

In 1809 Napoleon took Vaticanus to Paris as the spoils of war. It was returned to the Vatican in 1815. Between 1828 and 1838, Roman Catholic Cardinal Angelo Mai produced a typographical facsimile edition of Vaticanus which was not released until 1857. In 1843, Tischendorf was allowed to make a facsimile of a few verses.

In 1845, Samuel Tregelles was allowed to see Vaticanus briefly. He commented,

> "They would not let me open it without searching my pockets, and depriving me of pen, ink, and paper; and at the same time two prelati kept me in constant conversation in Latin, and if I looked at a passage too long, they would snatch the book out of my hand."

This of course was the period of history in which hostility between the Catholic Church existed toward Protestants. The authorities in Rome routinely obstructed Protestants scholars from other than cursory examination of Vaticanus. The exception to that was what seemed to be an unusually cozy relationship between the Catholic hierarchy and Constantine Tischendorf. He was allowed 42 hours over a period of three weeks to copy the New Testament text thereof.

In 1861 F. H .A. Scrivener commented,

> "Codex Vaticanus 1209 is probably the oldest large vellum manuscript in existence, and is the glory of the great Vatican Library in Rome. To these legitimate sources of deep interest must be added the almost romantic curiosity which has been excited by the jealous watchfulness of its official guardians, with whom an honest zeal for its safe preservation seems to have now degenerated into a species of capricious willfulness, and who have shewn a strange incapacity for making themselves the proper use of a treasure they scarcely permit others more than to gaze upon. It . . . is so jealously guarded by the Papal authorities that ordinary visitors see nothing of it but the red Morocco binding."[9]

See Appendix D for a listing of verses and phrases omitted from Vaticanus when compared to the Traditional Text.

The Initial Caps Issue

On February 17, 2015, the Vatican Library released a digitized, high-definition, photographic display of Vaticanus online.[10] Prior to this time, very few scholars had the privilege of carefully examining the manuscript apart from Vatican authorities and a few Protestant scholars of which the Vatican allowed very brief viewings. Most of the well-known textual editors of the past 150 years, including Westcott and Hort, never saw the detail which is available today. What they worked from were rather crude, black-and-white transcribed, typographical facsimiles printed with the technology of 19th century printing. That is, someone copied the text, specifically Cardinal Mai, which in turn was then used to set Greek type face and then printed by letterpress printing.[11] Scholars saw the reproduced printed text, but most never saw the details of the actual leaves of Vaticanus — until the year 2015. What is available today is revealing, to say the least.

Codex Vaticanus exhibits a literary phenomenon which is unique to a manuscript purportedly produced in the fourth century. At the beginning of *every* biblical book in Vaticanus, there is what is called in modern printing an "initial cap" which is also sometimes called a "drop cap." This paragraph commenced with an initial "drop cap." The initial cap at the beginning of this paragraph is similar schematically to what is found throughout Vaticanus.

Notice in figure 3, located near page 96 in chapter 5, that the initial drop cap marks the beginning of the Book of Hebrews. Also observe that the first word is πολυμερως (*polumeros*) and means "at sundry times." But notice also that the upper case Π is out in the margin and the rest of the word commences in the interior of the text.

Moreover, the initial caps found in Vaticanus are clearly painted in bright colors. There is additional colored artwork at the beginning of each biblical book. What is significant about this is that such artwork is clearly medieval in character. Though the artwork above the beginning of each book certainly could have been added long after the original manuscript was produced, the initial drop caps are integral to the text. That is, the initial drop cap had to have been created when the manuscript was prepared. But they clearly are medieval in character. In every case, the first letter of the first word of the first chapter of each book begins with such an initial drop cap. That first letter is missing in the main text body of each biblical book. In a few cases, it seems that first letter of the text body might have been scratched out. But upon closer examination, what is in view is bleed-through from text on the other side of the parchment leaf. For each biblical book of the Bible in Vaticanus, there is an initial drop cap in the margin followed immediately by the next letter of the text in regular size in the text body.

For example, many of the Pauline epistles of the New Testament begin with the word *Paul*. Thus in Ephesians 1:1, the text begins, "Paul, an apostle of Jesus Christ by the will of God . . .." Therefore, in Vaticanus, the first letter of the first word is the upper case Greek letter for "P" which is Π (*pi*). It is in the margin to the left of the text body in a large, colorful, decorative letter of medieval artwork. In the text body the next letter is the smaller, normal text-body sized Greek letter for "a which is "α" (*alpha*). And of course, the remainder of the word *Paulos* (i.e., Paul in English) and thus the book commences. What is clearly apparent is that the initial drop cap is integral to the text body. That is, the drop cap was written when the rest of the text was written. But it is clearly medieval in its character.

What is implicit is that Vaticanus was either (1) written altogether at some medieval time, or (2) it was modified and re-written then.

Other ancient manuscripts dating to the fourth and fifth centuries either have no textual artwork whatsoever or what little there is are simply "curly q" doodles in black ink, almost always at the end of a book where there was a little space left over on the parchment. In no other ancient documents of the fourth and fifth centuries that this author has researched is there colored textual artwork or drop caps, particularly integral to the text.

Full-color, initial drop caps as a literary device were unknown in the time frame when Vaticanus was purported to have been produced. Once again, the artwork of the initial drop caps in Vaticanus is clearly medieval in character.[12]

From this simple observation, the implication is profound. Vaticanus lacks textual integrity. It is either of relatively late production in medieval times, or it was re-worked and re-written in medieval times. In either case, it cannot be relied upon as an ancient copy of Scripture, Alexandrian or otherwise.

Minuscule Lettering

Let us briefly review some basic terminology of the New Testament textual debate. Greek lettering, dating back to at least the fourth century A.D. is called *uncial* lettering. It is writing WHICH IS ALL UPPER-CASE LETTERS. This is also know as *majescule* lettering. However, around the ninth and tenth centuries A.D., a form of cursive lettering or lower-case letters was developed which is known as *minuscule* lettering. Thus, a distinctive of a manuscript produced in the fourth century is that it will have all uncial (or upper case) lettering. A characteristic of manuscripts written in later medieval times will have minuscule (or lower case) lettering.

What is peculiar about Vaticanus is that portions of the codex (i.e., the volume) are written in minuscule lettering. Approximately, the first half of Genesis is in minuscule lettering and then the latter half continues in uncial letters.[13] The conventional answer to this observation is that the first half of Genesis was lost over the centuries and that later scribes re-copied those chapters utilizing minuscule lettering. However, the wonders of high definition digital color photography are telling. A close examination of the first half of Genesis and the second half shows the appearance of the parchment to be virtually identical. The minuscule portion looks no different than the uncial portion, suggesting there is not much, if any difference in their respective age. A different scribe is apparent for each section, but the parchment looks the same.

The same is true of the end of Vaticanus from midway in the Epistle of the Hebrews through the Book of Revelation. The end of the New Testament in Vaticanus is in minuscule lettering. What is curious is that the text art is substantially different than the rest of the New Testament. It frankly appears more ancient than the main body of the codex. There is an initial drop cap at the beginning of the Book of Revelation, but it is not integral to the text. It was clearly added after the fact, whereas the uncial portions of the rest of the codex had integral initial caps. Clearly a different scribe was involved and quite probably at a later time. But again, the parchment does not seem substantially different.

All of this leads to questions regarding the integrity of the text of Vaticanus. It clearly was not all produced at the same time. There certainly were several scribes involved in its production. It quite evidently was modified over the centuries.

Missing Books

Another anomaly found in Vaticanus is that the pastoral epistles of I & II Timothy and Titus, along with the little epistle of Philemon are omitted. This is not an issue of books missing at the end of the codex. The general epistles (Hebrews, James, I & II Peter, along with the epistles of John) are all included as well as the Revelation. And, there is not an apparent place where these epistles should have been in the volume. The pagination of the codex makes no allowance for them. Whoever produced the manuscript, for whatever reason, did not include these four epistles of the Apostle Paul.[14] The greater point, once again, is that Vaticanus is not a reliable source of the New Testament.

The foundational principle utilized by critical-text editors in weighting texts as to their importance suddenly is meaningless. Vaticanus and Sinaiticus have long been held up as the oldest and best manuscript evidence of the New Testament. In the case of Vaticanus, it is apparent that it is not ancient in its current state as displayed by the Vatican. At the least, it was doctored and decorated in medieval times, including the text body itself. Or, at the worst, it was recopied or produced altogether in medieval times. It thus is neither the oldest nor the best representation of the New Testament which is often repeated to this day. This is particularly so in the advertising and promotional material for modern language Bibles. Its claim to antiquity and thus its presumed textual integrity simply evaporates.

Inserted Pages

In several places in Vaticanus, the evidence is apparent that leaves (i.e., pages) have been inserted into the volume at some later date. This is evident in pages which are of different sized parchment and the parchment is of lighter coloration, indicating those particular pages were inserted at a later time. There seems to be a different scribe as well. This all points to those pages being of more recent age. This all goes to the greater evidence that Vaticanus does not have integrity. Over the centuries, unknown scribes or counterfeiters have monkeyed with it, greatly reducing its reliability as a primary source of ancient Scripture.

Changed Pagination

Vaticanus has a system of pagination in the upper and outer corner of each page. There are 1,536 pages in the codex. However, in the book of Acts, the pagination has been obviously overwritten or crossed out and a different and higher page number written above. This continues through much of the rest of the New Testament. What seems apparent is that a leaf was inserted into the main volume at some later date, muddling the original pagination. Once again, this is clear evidence that Vaticanus was tampered with and modified at some later date. Once again, the conclusion is that it has little integrity or reliability as an ancient source of Scripture.

Strange Anomalies

Throughout Vaticanus there are other strange anomalies which are difficult to explain. On an old document purportedly dating to the fourth century, one would expect there to be damage to the leaves such as worm holes — the proverbial book worms. And, indeed there are. One would expect the worms to not care if they munched their way through words and letters of the text on a given page. And, they did. But what is truly puzzling is that there are worm holes on pages and the text goes around the worm holes. The scribe copying or re-copying the text worked around holes in the parchment.

Now, this could have happened when the manuscript was originally produced. However, it would seem odd that a scribe in producing a brand new manuscript would not use fresh and intact parchment leaves. Upon consideration, this option seems highly unlikely — that a scribe would from the get go use defective parchment leaves. Moreover, there are many such places where the scribe wrote around holes in the parchment.

Another possibility which the textual establishment likely will reject out of hand is that like Simonides and Sinaiticus, a medieval scribe used what was then a recently prepared codex to prepare what has come to be known as Vaticanus. He worked around the worm holes in the parchment as he came to them. This would explain how medieval artwork and initial drop caps integral to the text which are clearly medieval in character were placed in the text. This possibility certainly will be rejected by the critical text establishment, but it makes sense and answers other issues.

What is of further significance is that the numerous worm holes are isolated one from another. That is, a given worm hole will appear in a single leaf of parchment. However, it does not appear in the leaves prior or after the hole in one. What this clearly suggests is that the holes in the parchment leaves occurred prior to them being bound into the volume (i.e., codex). Scribes would do their work copying each page on a desk specially designed for that purpose. Then, the leaf would be set apart for the ink to dry. At some point thereafter, the leaves would be assembled together into the beginnings of a volume. But the point is that the worm holes had to be present prior to the assembly of the leaves together. This would again lend itself to the idea of a scribe at some later time copying the manuscript on secondary parchment. Implied is what we call Vaticanus was not the primary document produced in the fourth century, but a manuscript produced at a later time.

Other anomalies in the text are not a few small rectangular holes in the parchment. They surely were not done by book worms. This author cannot offer even a speculative reason.

Overwriting

In examining every page of Vaticanus, it is apparent that there are some areas where there is overwriting with India ink. That is, a modern scribe took it upon himself to write over what was originally there. This is evident in several places suggesting a later scribe modified the text. The significance of this again suggests that Vaticanus is not a reliable source of ascertaining the text of the New Testament. It is flawed on numerous levels.

Conclusion

Burgon certainly was right. More than 160 years ago, he proclaimed Vaticanus to be one of the most corrupt manuscripts of the New Testament to exist. Close examination of it today surely shows his assessment to be true. There is every indication that what exists today was at the least reworked in medieval times, if not produced altogether then. In the next chapter compelling evidence will be presented that Vaticanus was significantly modified as late as the 19th century, in a clear effort to deceive and distort basic doctrine.

Whether the reader accepts all of these allegations or not is beside the point. The point is that there is more than reasonable doubt to conclude that Vaticanus is neither an honest nor accurate record of the New Testament.

End Notes:

1. John Burgon, *Inspiration and Interpretation,* (London: J. H. & Jas. Parker, 1861); reprint, Collinswood, Jersey: Bible for Today, 1984, p. 74 (citation is to reprint edition).

2. Ibid.

3. Ibid., p. 77.

4. Scrivener, Frederick Henry Ambrose; Edward Miller (1894). *A Plain Introduction to the Criticism of the New Testament.* 1 (4 ed.). London: George Bell & Sons. p. 114

5. John Burgon, *The Revision Revised*, London: John Murray, Albemarle Street, 1883, p. 9.

6. T. C. Skeat, "The Codex Sinaiticus, the Codex Vaticanus and Constantine," Journal of Theological Studies 50 (1999), pp. 583–625.

7. Bruce M. Metzger, *Manuscripts of the Greek Bible: An Introduction to Greek Palaeography*, New York, Oxford: Oxford University Press, 1991, p. 74.

8. I John 5:7 "For there are three that bear record in heaven, the Father, the Word, and the Holy Ghost: and these three are one." Vaticanus and most editions of the modern Critical Text omit most of this verse from the New Testament. For example, the ESV reads, "For there are three that testify." The full Traditional Text reading is "For there are three that bear record in heaven, the Father, the Word, and the Holy Ghost: and these three are one."

9. Frederick Henry Ambrose Scrivener. *Six Lectures on the Text of the New Testament and the Ancient Manuscripts*. Cambridge, 1875, p. 26.

10. http://digi.vatlib.it/view/MSS_Vat.gr.1209

11. Tischendorf was also allowed to produce a printed facsimile edition in cooperation and collusion with Cardinal Mai in 1867.

12. The blog of the British Library http://blogs.bl.uk/digitised manuscripts/2015/03/greek-manuscripts-digitisation -project-the-final-seventy-five-manuscripts-go-online.html does show text art and initial caps similar to that found in Vaticanus. However, in *every* illustration provided of such textual art or initial caps, that dating was medieval, ranging from the 11th to 16th centuries. Such text art simply does not exist as early as the 4th century.

13. Recall, that both Vaticanus and Sinaiticus are manuscripts of the entire Bible as well as books of the Apocrypha. Though the New Testament portions are what are salient to the debate, from a literary perspective, the entire codex is significant.

14. This is evidently why Kurt Aland thought that the pastoral epistles were not authentic.

CHAPTER EIGHT

THE LAST TWELVE VERSES OF MARK

No doubt the most infamous irregularity of both Vaticanus and Sinaiticus is the omission of the last twelve verses of Mark (Mark 16:9-20). These verses are the clear description of the resurrection of Christ in the Gospel of Mark. A favorite theory of higher criticism is that the Gospel of Mark was the first Gospel written and that the others, Matthew and Luke particularly (the other synoptic Gospels), were later embellishments based upon Mark. Higher critical theory further postulates that Matthew and Luke fabricated the resurrection accounts and only Mark's account, the account minus the resurrection, is the correct one. The finger prints of the evil one upon this insidious scheme should be all too apparent. But the fact is, Mark 16:9-20 was deleted from the main body of the Gospel of Mark in Vaticanus and Sinaiticus. The evidence will show the deletion was in recent times.

Though these 12 verses appear in thousands of other manuscripts, we are told that because Vaticanus and Sinaiticus are the two (allegedly) oldest, largely intact copies of the Bible in existence, they must be weighted as most authoritative over the thousands of other manuscripts which are not as old. Thus, in virtually all modern versions of the Bible, there is a footnote or marginal note saying these 12 verses are not found in the two oldest and best manuscripts. Though included in most modern Bible versions, a question is left for the reader, “Yea hath God said?” Is this really part of the Word of God? Is this really part of the Bible? And, these are not just any 12 verses, they describe in precise detail the resurrection of Jesus Christ and then His Great Commission. If the devil could choose 12 verses to remove from the Bible, what more powerful ones could he choose? The resurrection of Jesus Christ authenticates Jesus as the Son of God (Romans 1:1). It is the victory over not only death, but the devil himself. (I Corinthians 15). And then, if the devil could convince the world that the other gospels were mere embellishments upon the Gospel of Mark, and the true copy of Mark did not contain the resurrection account, Satan hoped he could erase it from history.

But Satan forgot that there are about 6,000 other manuscripts of the Traditional Text out there which all clearly describe the resurrection of Christ, not only in Mark, but all through the New Testament. It is the keystone of Christian doctrine.

But let’s look more carefully at Vaticanus and the end of the Gospel of Mark. The story becomes very interesting.

The Conventional Wisdom

The conventional wisdom once again is that Vaticanus and Sinaiticus are two ancient, independent witnesses of the original text of the New Testament. The notion continues, they are similar in that they are of about the same antiquity (the fourth century) and that they are of Alexandrian origin. Therefore, we must weight them as being more important than the thousands of later traditional-text manuscripts. This is the conventional wisdom of the Critical Text.

However, as we have seen throughout this volume, the conventional wisdom has been consistently wrong. We shall see that Vaticanus and Sinaiticus are not independent witnesses, but in fact were modified at the same time by the same scribe in the same way. Their independent testimony suddenly becomes collusion and their integrity as evidence suddenly becomes dishonesty.

The Same Scribe for Mark 16 in Vaticanus and Sinaiticus

As incredulous as this may seem, it is true. The portion of the Gospel of Mark 16 in both Vaticanus and Sinaiticus were written out by the same scribe. Tischendorf refers to him as "Scribe D." As remarkable as it may seem, even Tischendorf himself noticed this and commented about it on several occasions.[1]

Volumes such as Vaticanus and Sinaiticus were written upon parchment leaves, but each leaf was actually part of a quire. That is, one larger leaf was folded over to make leaves of four to eight pages (one page on each side of each fold). Thus for the last 12 verses of Mark 16 to be omitted required that an entire quire be modified. Is there any evidence that such happened? Indeed there is.

Drs. Tischendorf and Harris

First, on the pages of the quire of the immediate vicinity of Mark 16, a different scribe was involved. As noted above, he is called Scribe D. As noted below, a Dr. Harris referred to him as Scribe B. They are one and the same. He is also the same scribe who wrote Mark 16 of Sinaiticus.

In 1893, a British literary scholar by the name of James Harris wrote of this very issue. It is instructive. He said:

> "It is generally held today that Tischendorf was justified in recognizing in the Sinaitic Codex the traces of the same hand as wrote the New Testament portion of the Codex Vaticanus. As this is a most important point, and one that settles, if it be correctly inferred, both the unity of time and of place in the two Codices, I spend a few moments in the statement of the case.
>
> According to Tischendorf there are in the Codex Sinaiticus six cancel [replaced] leaves of the New Testament which have been rewritten by another hand . . .. The evidence for this is Tischendorf's eyes and Tischendorf's judgment. The hands are apparently the same, and there are concurrent peculiarities in spelling, etc., which persuade the judgment to finally identify [sic]. There is nothing unreasonable in the occasional change from one scribe to another when they are occupied on the same book. It is *a priori* likely enough.
>
> On such a matter, Tischendorf's opinion is of the greatest weight; he did not know much about

> papyrus hands or cursive hands, but he knew more about vellum-uncial hands than anybody else. Consequently most people, even if they have not seen the Sinaitic Codex, accept his judgment. But after Tischendorf had come to his conclusion he took the argument a step further, and said that the hand in question was the same hand that wrote the New Testament portion of the Vatican Codex. The argument is as before a palaeographical one and depends on shapes of letters, spellings, etc.
>
> Dr. Hort, who completely accepted Tischendorf's judgment, remarked that its accuracy was confirmed by the fact that the six cancel [replaced] leaves were conjugate [adjacent] leaves in the quire, so that they were really three double leaves. This is as it should be, for in a MS. in which the quire is the foundation, one cannot cancel [replace] a single leaf... .
>
> The interest of the question is much intensified by the fact that one of the cancelled [replaced] leaves is that which contains the closing passages of S. Mark, where both Aleph [Sinaiticus] and B [Vaticanus] show a remarkable omission. The coincidence is a curious one, and many people, naturally enough, refuse to believe that it is accidental. They say we have the scribe of B [Vaticanus] twice over for the omission, and not two separate authorities."[2] *[Editors note: words in brackets have been inserted to help understand British/archaic or technical terms. Underlining added.]*

What Dr. Harris says in his scholarly tones is that the same scribe rewrote the final portion of Mark 16 in both Vaticanus and Sinaiticus which omit the last 12 verses. Moreover, this was accomplished by replacing six leaves at the end of Mark in each codex respectively.

Furthermore, it was Tischendorf himself who first brought this to light. Dr. Harris concludes by noting that many scholars of his day believe that this was neither coincidence nor accident. In other words, it was intentional. Harris does not go on to speculate as to by whom, how, or why this was done. We shall launch into those waters shortly. But once again, there is clear evidence that Vaticanus was modified, quite apparently in collusion with Sinaiticus to advance a particular heretical view — a denial of the resurrection of Jesus Christ by omitting it from what higher criticism considered to be the primary source gospel — the Gospel of Mark.

What is ironic indeed is that though Tischendorf was the first to point this out, albeit in Latin in the introduction when he published a printed version of Vaticanus in 1867 and then again in Latin in the prologue of a later Greek New Testament published in 1884, both published in Leipzig, the rest of the scholarly world of textual criticism conveniently ignored it. Dr. James Rendel Harris was considered a world class scholar of biblical literature who was a professor, lecturer, and author of at least 17 rather technical, scholarly literary works in the latter part of the 19th and first part of the 20th centuries. He confirmed Tischendorf's conclusion regarding the replacement of the leaves at the end of Mark in both Vaticanus and Sinaiticus by the same scribe. But he too was ignored by the liberal textual establishment of the day.

The Forensic Evidence

Enter once again the wonders of modern, digital, high-definition photography. If one will carefully examine the final portion of

Vaticanus and Sinaiticus (especially the Hendrickson facsimile edition), one will notice that the parchment leaves of those quires are slightly lighter in coloration. To this observer, that indicates they are of more recent vintage than the rest of the leaves of the text before and after. That is forensic evidence and it only confirms what Tischendorf rather surprisedly noticed. James Harris seconded the motion.

Codex Alexandrinus

Interestingly, Codex Alexandrinus was another ancient manuscript of the New Testament and as its name implies was produced at Alexandria, Egypt. It later found its way to Constantinople and then, amazingly to Mount Athos, near Thessalonika, Greece.[3] It purportedly dates to the fifth century. However, Codex Alexandrinus contains the last 12 verses of Mark. If the conventional dating of Vaticanus and Sinaiticus is to be believed, they are not much older than Alexandrinus. Yet, Alexandrinus is a manuscript from Alexandria, no less, which contains the last 12 verses of Mark. It seems strange if the true New Testament did not contain the last 12 verses of Mark 16, why does a cousin manuscript of almost the same age and the same place of origin contain it? Was the doctrine of the resurrection of Christ invented a few decades later in, of all places, Alexandria, Egypt — the locus of Gnostic theology in the Mediterranean world of that day? Let the reader decide.

Stichometry

Here is a word most people have never heard of. But in the context of literature and textual matters, it is a technical term which pertains to the actual construction of lines of text. It was a textual discipline used in the world and the time of professional scribes.[4] Yet, in the debate over the last twelve verses of Mark 16, stichometry will become of importance. Stichometry is the measure of letter sizes, space sizes and frequency, the number of letters to a line, the number of lines and columns to a page.[5]

At the end of the Gospel of Mark in Vaticanus (as well as in Sinaiticus) there is a glaring blank space where the last 12 verses should have been. Whoever recopied those pages *without* them had to know exactly how much space to allow so that when the Gospel of Luke commenced it was precisely where it should be. This is where stichometry comes in. The scribe had to count the number of lines involved, along with the number of words and the number of letters to leave no more and no less room from Mark 16:8 to where Luke 1:1 commenced. And then the quire at the end of Mark 16 also included pages at the beginning of Luke 1. The scribe who recopied had to match those words on those lines exactly so that when the new section was inserted, it would match up precisely with the older section. Is there evidence that happened? Indeed there is.

Vaticanus is laid out with three columns of text per page. Mark 16:8 ends about three quarters of the way down the second column. The rest of that column and the third column on that page are blank. That is the exact space needed for the last 12 verses of Mark 16. On the next following page, Luke 1 commences. In any other book of the

Bible in Vaticanus that much blank space is not wasted. If the Gospel of Mark had ended where it now does, the Gospel of Luke would have commenced at the top of the third column, not wasting almost a page and a half of valuable parchment space.

A similar phenomenon occurs in Sinaiticus. Codex Sinaiticus rather has four columns per page and the letter size is a little smaller. But low and behold, four lines into the second column where Mark 16:8 ends, there is a blank space which extends to the bottom of the page. This again is exactly the necessary space for the last 12 verses of Mark 16. At least in Sinaiticus, the scribe re-working the text did not waste the rest of the page, but commenced Luke 1 at the top of the third column.

The point is simple. In both Vaticanus and Sinaiticus, there conveniently are blank spaces where Mark 16:9-20 should have been. The pages respectively were re-copied and those 12 verses were intentionally omitted. As noted above, the quire leaves of both volumes for Mark 16 and vicinity were replaced and completely recopied for each codex and the same scribe did the work on each.

The intrigue of who did this, why and when, is an amazing mystery. We will venture some educated guesses a little later in this chapter. But the overarching point is that Vaticanus was intentionally modified to omit one of the foundational truths of Christianity — the resurrection of Jesus Christ. Apart from that flagrant heresy, Vaticanus has no textual integrity as a primary source for the New Testament. The modern Critical Text is built upon a manuscript intentionally modified to deceive.

The Saga of Manuscript 2427

At the University of Chicago library lies a telling manuscript. Originally, known as the Goodspeed Ms. 38, it also came to be known as "Archaic Mark." Then it came to be known as MS 2427 (i.e., Manuscript 2427). Today, its library reference number is shelf mark 972. It is acknowledged by all, including the University of Chicago, to have been produced in the 19th century.[6] It is a verbatim copy of Vaticanus' Gospel of Mark — word for word, letter for letter. But it is very cleverly done giving the appearance of great antiquity. However, modern analytical processes have demonstrated it to be of modern production. Chemical analysis showed that one of its inks was not invented until sometime in the 19th century. It is thus a forgery. Yet, the University of Chicago keeps it as an example of a forged document, purporting to be ancient.

However, the ancient appearance of MS 2427 was such that even Kurt Aland, renowned German textual expert, proclaimed it to be a "category l" manuscript. But here is what is amazing. MS 2427 included the last 12 verses of Mark 16 whereas the purported original does not. How could that be?

The answer is as simple as it is profound. MS 2427 was copied from Vaticanus *before* the last 12 verses of Mark were removed. We thus have *prima facie* evidence of what the complete Gospel of Mark in Vaticanus looked like before it was intentionally modified. The evidence is clear. The last 12 verses of Mark were removed from Vaticanus (and most likely from Sinaiticus) at some point during the mid 19th century.

Who, Why, and How?

There is no smoking gun as to who did the modifying of Vaticanus (or Sinaiticus). But let us consider several thoughts. These alterations took place quite apparently sometime during the mid-19th century. That is when MS 2427 was produced with its full reading of Mark 16. Simonides had completed his work of Sinaiticus by 1840 (which included all of Mark). Roman Catholic prelate Cardinal Angelo Mai published an official facsimile edition of Vaticanus in 1857 which did *not* include the last 12 verses of Mark 16.

Therefore, who in that period of history had interest to undercut the historic Christian doctrine of the resurrection of Christ? There probably were cults and other fringe groups who might be inclined to that end. But a major group in Europe particularly was the German Rationalist movement which questioned or denied just about anything miraculous in New Testament Christianity. They certainly had an intellectual motive to undercut the resurrection for it was both the foundation and keystone of orthodox Christian doctrine. However, whether any German Rationalist had the skill, expertise, or resources to accomplish such a task is questionable. Though Tischendorf showed himself to be of questionable integrity in much of the greater saga of the discovery of Sinaiticus and even Vaticanus, the fact that he was surprised that the last 12 verses of Mark were missing from Vaticanus would seem to exonerate him from such deviousness.

There is another group across Europe which for centuries did have the skills, expertise, and resources to accomplish such a task. That was the Jesuits. As the principal agents of the Counter Reformation, their history is replete with a long rap sheet of producing forgeries, fake documents, and altering documents to further the goals and polices of the Vatican. They also were renowned for infiltrating Protestant churches, institutions of higher learning, and other Protestant organizations, often working as a fifth column within. The Oxford Movement in England is one example. Through such infiltration, they reportedly were the original agents of the German Rationalist movement and higher criticism. Their objective was to undermine confidence in the "paper pope" of the Protestants — Sola Scriptura — which was their Traditional Text Bibles.

Could it be that in the 10 or 12 years after Simonides had finished his work on what came to be known as Sinaiticus and after Vaticanus became largely known, that agents of the Jesuits, perhaps posing as higher critics, undertook the tasks of altering Vaticanus and Sinaiticus to further their ends? Cardinal Mai certainly was involved in the publishing of Vaticanus and helped facilitate Tischendorf and his work with Sinaiticus. That is verifiable history. Though the Catholic Church has always recognized the resurrection of Christ, many Rationalists did not.

Or, perhaps the goal was to undermine confidence in the Bible itself by producing purportedly ancient manuscripts which undercut the resurrection. Protestants therefore could only look to the traditions of Rome and her Vulgate Bible. And that was one of the objectives of the counter-Reformation all along. This obviously is speculation and we likely will never know. But it makes sense. Cardinal Mai pops up all through the mid-19th century history of Vaticanus and Sinaiticus. German Rationalism, of which Tischendorf was a part, sought to undermine historic Christian doctrine and faith in the

Traditional Text. Perhaps these two forces colluded together. The Jesuits certainly had the expertise and ability. The Rationalists in Tischendorf certainly had an inside track to seemingly old manuscripts. They would make a potent team.

But the bottom line is that Vaticanus was intentionally altered, most likely in the mid 19th century by agents willing to undercut the resurrection of Christ. That in itself should negate any confidence in it as a source of Scripture.

End Notes:

1. Constantine von Tischendorf's *Novum Testamentum Graece, Volumen III*, Prolegomena scripsit Casparus Renatus Gregory (Lipsiae 1884), pp. 345-6, 360. See also *Novum Testamentum Vaticanum. Post Angeli Maii Aloirumque Imperfectos Labores ex ipso Codice* (Lipsiae 1867), pp. XXI-XXIII, in which he discusses the matter at greater length.

2. James Rendel Harris, *Stichometry* (London 1893), pp. 73-74. From pp. 71-89 in an appendix to his book, entitled'On the Common Origin of the Codices Aleph [Sinaiticus] and B [Vaticanus]'Harris provides greater detail about Scribe D. In a lecture he gave at Mansfield College, Oxford, on the 6th of June 1893, Harris concluded that the identity of Sinaiticus' Scribe D with Vaticanus' Scribe B demonstrate that both mss. were of the same age and produced in the same scriptorium by the same scribe.

3. F. C. Burkitt, *Codex Alexandrinus*, Journal of Theological Studies XI, (1909-1910), pp. 603-606.

4. Recall that prior to the advent of the moveable type printing press in the mid 15th century, all documents, manuscripts, and literature of whatever type were hand copied by scribes. It was a profession in the fullest sense of the word, on a par with lawyers and doctors. With the proliferation of mechanical printing of whatever form, the profession of scribes faded away

to extinction.

5. Bill Cooper, *The Forging of Codex Sinaiticus* (Kindle Locations 1101-1102).

6. M.M. Mitchell & Duncan PA. *Chicago's Archaic Mark (MS 2427):* "A reintroduction to its enigmas and a fresh collation of its readings." *Novum Testamentum*, Volume 48, 2006 as noted by Bill Cooper, *The Forging of Codex Sinaiticus*.

CHAPTER NINE
CONCLUSION

As we have examined the history and evidence which pertain to Sinaiticus and Vaticanus, it is apparent that Sinaiticus is not old and that Vaticanus has been altered. In both cases, it seems apparent that the intent was to deceive.

Sinaiticus: Tischendorf versus Simonides

To summarize, the track record of Constantine von Tischendorf has been shown to be one of deception and duplicity. Few in the world of ancient Mediterranean literature today believe his claim of finding portions of what came to be known as Codex Sinaiticus lying in a wastebasket waiting to be used as kindling. To this day, the authorities at St. Catherine's Greek Monastery at Mount Sinai deny that ever happened. The British Library which presently has possession of much of the manuscript is strangely silent about such an escapade. They will not dignify the claim by even mentioning it in their official history of its provenance.

It is apparent that Tischendorf lied to the authorities at Mount Sinai in 1859 in promising to return the rest of the manuscript if they would loan it to him. He never did return it and it is apparent he had no intention of ever doing so. Tischendorf thereafter pawned off what he called Codex Sinaiticus to a gullible world as a fourth-century copy of the Bible.

To the contrary, a Greek paleographer/calligrapher by the name of Constantine Simonides plainly said he wrote Sinaiticus between 1839 and 1840. His claim was immediately derided and dismissed by the academic and textual elite, particularly of England. Yet, Simonides persisted in the face of overwhelming opposition. His character was defamed and he was routinely accused of forging other ancient documents and manuscripts. In fact, he came to be known, to this day, as Simonides the forger. Yet, the one document which he plainly said he had produced was denied, while his critics accused him of forging everything else he had ever got his hands on. His critics seemed to have missed the irony of their charges.

As that controversy waxed on, Simonides publicly challenged Tischendorf to a public debate and at the same time to produce Sinaiticus. Simonides would then point out personal acrostics and other internal identifying marks. Tischendorf refused. Coincidentally, not long thereafter the very pages on which Simonides had left personal markings and which would vindicate him, came up missing. That is a strange coincidence. It rather points to evidence being destroyed.

Simonides then produced a witness by the name of Kallinokos who corroborated his claim. When surrogates of Tischendorf claimed that

Kallinokos did not even exist, further proof was forthcoming verifying his existence and veracity.

The long and the short of it is that all the evidence demonstrated the veracity of Simonides on the one hand and the devious character of Tischendorf on the other.

Sinaticus: Dating

The crux of this whole issue comes down to the dating of Codex Sinaiticus. What is ironic indeed is that after all the controversy and politically-correct debate are peeled away, the primary source alleging that Sinaiticus dates to the fourth century is Constantine von Tischendorf, and him alone. His principal methodology of dating was paleography which by its very nature is highly subjective. Though several others such as Samuel Tregelles and Henry Bradshaw supported Tischendorf's claim, there is no evidence that they ever saw the actual manuscript itself. Rather, they only saw printed facsimiles thereof which are useless insofar as paleographic dating is concerned. The British Library to this day claims no other means of dating the manuscript.

And so, the dating of Sinaiticus comes down to the veracity of Tischendorf over Simonides. The former has a documented track record of duplicity and lack of integrity. Though Simonides was routinely accused of forgery, no specific instance has ever been proven. Those who knew the man personally defended his integrity.

The physical forensic evidence as well as the textual issues of Hermas and Barnabas all deny the antiquity of Sinaiticus.

Sinaiticus: Motives

In stepping back and considering who had a motive or what that motive might be, there are insights. It is clear that a relatively obscure, young, research scholar by the name of Constantine Tischendorf became Dr. Constantine von Tischendorf as a result of his "discoveries" of Sinaiticus and Vaticanus. He was awarded gold medals, and additional honorary degrees and in the process became not only famous but also wealthy as well. Tischendorf had a powerful motive in denying the claims of Simonides. His work, particularly with Sinaiticus, had made him a wealthy and famous man. Simonides claims directly threatened his fame and fortune and therefore had to be stopped.

Moreover, by the mid 1860s, the development of the "new" Greek text of Westcott and Hort, based almost exclusively upon Vaticanus and Sinaiticus, was well underway. There was much academic and intellectual hubris on the line. To admit that Sinaiticus was not ancient but of recent origin would be a major embarrassment to the developing critical-text establishment. Tischendorf was a part of that establishment. Hence, there was another powerful motive to impugn Simonides and his claim that Sinaiticus was only 20 years old.

On the other hand, what motive did Simonides have in forcing the issue of Sinaiticus? He was already highly regarded in literary circles across Europe. He stood to gain nothing financially from his claim of having produced Sinaiticus. He knew he would be ridiculed and pilloried for undercutting the party line of the critical-text establishment. Simonides had nothing to gain and much to lose. And, that is exactly what happened. He went from being highly regarded as a paleographer and expert on ancient documents to the opprobrium of "Simonides the forger."

Some have claimed that his motive was retaliation against Tischendorf for pressing charges against him in Germany in 1855. (Those charges were dismissed by the German authorities.) Yet, such alleged retaliation did not occur until five years later. Moreover, it was thc British press which originally "broke" the story of the recent dating of Sinaiticus independently of Simonides. It was only after he was attacked in *The Guardian* newspaper by Hort and Tregelles that he publically responded in detail.

Simonides knew he would face fierce opposition and character assassination for his claims and that is exactly what happened. He therefore really had no motive in claiming to have written Sinaiticus other than trying to set the record straight.

Tischendorf, on the other hand, had powerful motives for impugning Simonides and his claims. Simonides had little or nothing to gain in claiming Sinaiticus as his own work other than trying to retain the honor of his name. Other than that, he had no motive in accusing Tischendorf of being less than honest.

Sinaiticus: Forensic Evidence

Only in recent years has the general public readily been able to have access in viewing Sinaiticus at the British Library through the development of high-definition, digital photography over the internet. Other manuscripts dating to the fourth or fifth centuries A.D. clearly show their age, having a bronzed or brown patina to the coloration of their pages. However, to this day, Sinaiticus has the appearance of off-white. In fact, Russian scholars which saw the portion not long after it arrived at the University of Leipzig remarked that the manuscript was "snow white." That is strange for a document which supposedly was more than 1,500 years old. But it is not strange at all if the manuscript had been produced only several decades earlier. That is smoking-gun evidence. All other manuscripts from the fourth or fifth centuries are brown or very tan in their appearance. Sinaiticus is still white, though quite apparently somewhat "antiqued" to make it seem older. All the fingerprints of a counterfeit are present. And, indeed, it remains a counterfeit being presented as an ancient manuscript when in fact it is not.

Sinaiticus: Textual Difficulties

As was noted in some detail in chapter six, there are words found throughout Sinaiticus, especially in the appendage books of the *Shepherd of Hermas* and the *Epistle of Barnabas*, which are Latinisms – that is words which are of Latin derivation which were unknown and unused in the fourth century. Simonides said he worked from an exemplar called the Moscow Edition. Little or nothing is known about this document, but (1) it clearly was Alexandrian in its text type, and (2) it was much later dating because of the usage of Greek words based upon much later Latin words as well as some Greek words which were of late usage and not Koine Greek (i.e., ancient Greek). These preclude Sinaiticus from having been produced in the fourth century. Its exemplar, the Moscow Edition, dates to relatively recent modern times. Once again another smoking gun is evident precluding Sinaiticus from originating in the fourth century.

The inescapable conclusion is that Sinaiticus is not old. And, it certainly is not the oldest. Hence one of the basic pillars of the modern critical text crumbles before us.

Vaticanus

The history of Codex Vaticanus is not as dramatic or colorful as the 19th century history of Sinaiticus. But as was detailed in chapter seven, Vaticanus has issues which unravel the assumption that it is the best available representation of the New Testament. It clearly was altered at some point in medieval history, or at least made to look like medieval work.

Vaticanus: Drop Caps

Initial drop caps are a literary device used by scribes in the middle ages to decorate the copied page (and later by printers on the printed page). This author and researcher has not been able to locate any initial drop caps in biblical manuscripts (or manuscripts of any kind) going back as early as the fourth century. It simply did not exist then. Morever, the initial drop caps found throughout Vaticanus are (1) clearly medieval in the character of their artwork, and (2) are in every case integral to the text. That is, they were added to the manuscript at the same time the text was copied. Or to put that another way, the manuscript was produced at some point during medieval times (or made to look that way at even later times). This is powerful evidence contravening the alleged date of fourth century production.

Other Textual Anomalies

There are other textual anomalies throughout Vaticanus which mitigate against its integrity as a reliable, trustworthy ancient source of Scripture. Portions of it were written in minuscule writing which did not come on the scene until around the tenth century. There is evidence of pages being inserted into the text. The pagination of the volume in the New Testament has clearly been modified indicating that pages have been inserted which fouled up the original pagination system. There are missing books in the interior of the New Testament (not at the end of the manuscript) and were not included in the original pagination. There are places where there is clear evidence of overwriting by a later scribe. None of these anomalies, perhaps are conclusive in themselves, but together, they add up to a manuscript which is unreliable and corrupt. As Dean John Burgon wrote 150 years ago, Vaticanus is one of the most corrupt manuscripts to exist.

Vaticanus: The Last 12 Verses of Mark 16

Perhaps the most damning evidence of all is the fact the last 12 verse of Mark 16, which is Marks's account of the resurrection, were *purposefully* omitted. Furthermore, there is a blank space on the page where they should be. Close examination and applying the discipline of stichometry — the counting of letters, words, and lines — shows that there is the exact right amount of blank space at the end of Mark 16:8 for the final 12 verses. But they were intentionally omitted. The resurrection account was intentionally removed from the Gospel of Mark.

Moreover, the same scribe who did this deed at the end of Mark 16 was one and the same scribe who did so at the end of Sinaiticus. There clearly was collusion and a brazen attempt to deceive.

Vaticanus is the principal manuscript underlying the modern critical text. Its obvious problems and the clear intent to deceive, by whomever modified it, should make it useless as a primary source of the New Testament. It clearly is neither the oldest nor the best manuscript. Thus, the other major pillar of the modern critical text crumbles.

Final Implications

The implications of this are profound. Virtually all modern Bible versions are based wholly or substantially upon the modern Critical Text. And the vast majority of the Critical Text is based upon Vaticanus and Sinaiticus. If the basic source texts are corrupt, deceptive, and unreliable, that does not lend credence to the many modern translations which are based thereupon. This includes such modern and popular versions of the Bible as the NIV, the ESV, the NASB, the NRSV, the TEV and on and on. They all are based upon a corrupt foundation.

The Solution

So what is the solution to the problem? It is very simple. A return to the time-honored, venerable Traditional Text of the New Testament. It is so-called because it has been the basic text of the New Testament back to the mists of antiquity of the early church. (See chapter two for a brief rehearsal of its history.)

The earliest extant translations of the New Testament are all based upon the Traditional Text, later to be called the Received Text (i.e., Textus Receptus in Latin). From the Peshitta translation, produced in A.D. 150 and still used by the Syrian church, to *all* the Reformation era Bible translations, *all* were based upon the traditional Received Text. The Traditional Text was clearly the working text of the various church groups down through the ages, particularly Bible-believing churches.[1]

Though *complete* manuscript evidence of the Traditional Text may not extend back to the earliest centuries of Christianity, the translational evidence certainly does. Morever, it is not just aberrant anomalies of church history, but rather the mainstream of Bible-believing churches. The simple fact is that the Traditional Text of the New Testament has been the working text through the first 18 centuries of Bible translations. That is not insignificant. To the contrary, that is powerful evidence of which text has been used of God down through the ages.

It was only in the 19th century into the 20th century that intellectual pride and scholarly elitism informed us that two manuscripts were the oldest and best and should therefore take precedence and priority over the thousands of traditional-text manuscripts, unanimously accepted by the various Bible-preaching churches of Jesus Christ from the second century until the latter part of the 18th century.

Yet, as this book has documented, those two manuscripts are neither the oldest nor best. They are essentially counterfeits. Though the production of Sinaiticus by Simonides was never intended to deceive anyone, it has been manipulated and contrived to appear ancient. Its handlers certainly have sought to deceive. And, the evidence regarding the antiquity and integrity of Vaticanus is that it is fraudulent on its face.

Ironically, these purportedly ancient manuscripts have been pawned off on an unsuspecting religious world, which has swallowed hook, line, and sinker the slick advertising line and mantra, that they are the oldest and best.

In the English language, the principal manifestation of the Traditional Text is the time-honored King James Version. The latter has had more copies printed over its 400 years of history than any other Bible in history – in fact, likely more than all the rest put together. It is the Word of God in the English language.

That either is a coincidence of history or perhaps God had something to do with it. This author is of the opinion that there are not coincidences in God's work and plan. There are few things more quintessential to the work of God than the inspiration, preservation, transmission, and publishing of His Word. We need only look across history to see which text and Bible God has manifoldly blessed. That is the Traditional Text of the New Testament manifested in the King James Bible.

End Note:

1.The Latin Vulgate Bible was the principal translation of the Roman Catholic Church from the time of Jerome in A.D. 382. However, what is not widely know is that Jerome did not work directly from Greek manuscripts, but rather his work was a revision of the *Vetus Latina*, which was a collection of biblical texts in old Latin. Though a number of vernacular translations of the Vulgate were produced during the time of the Reformation and onward, none of them nor the Vulgate itself has ever been given serious consideration by the vast majority of evangelical, Bible-believing Christianity.

Appendix A

The Full Statement of James Donaldson's Critique of the Sinaitic Hermas

James Donaldson, *A Critical History of Christian Literature and Christian Doctrine from the Death of the Apostles to the Nicene Council, Volume III The Apologists*, London, MacMillan and Company, 1874, p. 307-311.

"In 1856 appeared the first edition of a Greek text of the Pastor of Hermas, under the care of Anger and Dindorf. The manuscript from which it was taken was three leaves of a codex lately found in Mount Athos by Simonides, and a copy of all the rest except a small portion. In a short time, however, considerable doubts were thrown on the genuineness of this text.... Tischendorf's suspicions had also been aroused. On examining the manuscript, however, he believed it to be a genuine manuscript, and gave a new rescension of it in Dressel's Apostolical Fathers. He also wrote a dissertation, showing that the Greek, though not forged, must have been a re-translation from the Latin. His arguments seemed to himself to be most convincing, and he remarks at the conclusion of his essay: '*Non deerunt quidem qui etiam tot argumentorum conjunctorum vim subterfugiant: nimirum sunt qui probabilitatis certique sensum aut natura non habent aut studiis amiserunt, quique verum tanquam adversarium malunt convincere quam integro animo invenire.*'[1]

To the Sinaitic Bible which Tischendorf found is attached a portion of the *Pastor of Hermas* in Greek, substantially the same as that given in the Athos manuscript. The variations are comparatively slight. And almost all the arguments that were adduced against the Athos manuscript are adducible against the Sinaitic. Tischendorf's opinion, however, changed on his finding the agreement between the two texts. In his Notitia, p. 45, he wrote: 'I am glad to be able to communicate that the Leipzig text is derived not from middle-age studies but from the old original text. My opposite opinion is proved correct in so far as that the Leipzig text is disfigured by many corruptions, such as without doubt proceed from middle-age use of Latin.' And he repeats his belief that the Leipzig text is genuine in the Prolegomena to the *Novum Testamentum Sinaiticum*. The discovery of this manuscript [Codex Sinaiticus] does not however impair the force of the arguments which he employed; and as they are in the main applicable to the Sinaitic codex, they compel us to reject the Greek text of Hermas given there as spurious. The arguments may be divided into two classes; those which indicate that the Greek is of late origin, and those which tend to prove that the Greek text is derived from some Latin translation.

The late origin of the Greek is indicated by the occurrence of a great number of words unknown to the classical period, but common in later or modern Greek. Such are, βουνος,συμβιος (as wife), με (for μετα), πρωτοκθεδριεις, ισχυροποιω, κατεπιθμω, ασυγκρασια, καταξυμα, καταεπθυμω, εξακριβαζομαι and such like. The lateness of the Greek appears also from late forms; such as αγαθτατης, μεθισταναι, οιδας, αφιουσι (αφινουσιν in Sim. Greek), καπεκοπταν, ενεσκιρωμενοι, επιδιδουν,ετιθουν, beside ετθεσαν, εσκαν, λημψν, ελπιδαν, τιθω, and ηνοιζας, επιασα, χειραν, απλοτηταν, σαρκαν, συνιω, συνιει; and some modern Greek forms, such as κραταουσα for κρατουσα, have been corrected by the writer of the manuscript. The lateness of the Greek appears also in the absence of the optative and the frequent use of ινα after ερωταν, αξιω, αιτουμαι, εντελλομαι, αξιος, &c., generally with the subjunctive, never with the optative. We also find εαν joined with the indicative. Εισ is continually used for εν, as εξουσιν τοτον εισ τον πυργον. We have also παρα after comparatives, and peculiar constructions, as περιχαρης του ιδειν, σπουδαιος εις το γνοναι, απεγνωριθαι απω. And we have a neuter plural joined with a plural verb, κτνην ερχονται.

Most, if not all, of these peculiarities now mentioned, may be found in Hellenistic writings, especially the New Testament; and some of them may be paralleled even in classical writers. But if we consider that the portion which has now been examined is small, and that every page is filled with these peculiarities, the only conclusion to which we can come is, that the Greek is not the Greek of the at least first five centuries of the Christian era. There is no document written within that period which has half so many neo-Hellenic forms, taken page by page, as this Greek of the Pastor of Hermas.

The peculiarities which point out a Latin origin are the following: There are, first, a number of Latin words where you would naturally expect Greek. Such are συμελλιον κερβικαριον, λεντιον, καρπασινον. Then there is a considerable number of passages preserved to us in Greek by Origen and other writers. The Sinaitic

Greek differs often from this Greek, and agrees with the Latin translation, especially the Palatine. There is every probability, especially internal, that the Greek of the ancient writers is nearer the original than the Sinaitic.

Then there occurs this passage, ερεις δε Μαξιμω ιδου θλιψσις ερχεται. The common Latin translation is: '*Dices autem; ecce magna tribulatio venit.*' Now here there is no trace of the 'Μαξιμω.' But we find it in the Palatine, 'Dicis autem maximo: ecce tribulatio,' which Dressel changes into 'Dicis autem; maxima ecce tribulatio.' The Palatine accounts well for the origin of Μαξιμω in the Sinaitic Greek, but it is not possible to account for the common 'magna,' if Μαξιμω had been originally in the Greek.

All these examples have been taken from the Sinaitic Greek. But the arguments become tenfold stronger if the Sinaitic Greek is to stand or fall with the Athos Greek. And this must be, for they are substantially the same. No doubt some allowance must be made for the carelessness of transcribers, but after every allowance is made, there is enough to convict both texts of a late origin, and to make it extremely probable that both are translations from the Latin."

End Notes:

1. Translation: "There will no doubt be individuals who will be able to elude the force of even so many arguments joined together, to wit, those who have naturally no perception of what can be proved and is certain, or who have lost this perception by their party feelings, and who prefer refuting the truth as if it were an adversary to finding it out with unbiased mind."

Appendix B

A Technical Critique of the Sinaitic Epistle of Barnabas by James Donaldson

"The Greek of the first four chapters and a half . . .. contains many of the conjectural emendations previously proposed by scholars. The Greek of the first four chapters exhibits some peculiar phenomena. Several words of unusual formation such as ακριβευεθαι, ανθρωποποιντος, and παρεισδυσις, are found nowhere else. One word εκσφενδοναν, occurring in c. 2, is found in Suidas, without any meaning attached to it except in one MS., notorious for additions of its own. It is also found in Eustathius or Eumathius an erotic writer as late at least as the twelfth century, who uses the word when describing how a girl is hurled from a ship. The Greek of Tischendorf uses it in the sense of 'turning away,' a sense unknown to antiquity, but now common among the people of Greece. The Greek also contains two or three additions to the Latin translation, which seems to us out of place and bewildering. And the quotations which Clemens Alexandrinus makes from Barnabas do not agree in some points with the Tischendorf Greek. Thus Clemens has συλληπτορες where the Tischendorf Greek has βοηθοι. Clemens has also πεμψαι, according to the Greek idiom which requires the aorist for a single act, where the Tischendorf Greek has the present infinitive, as if misled by the Latin. These peculiarities lead one to suspect that we have in the Sinaitic Greek either a very corrupt MS. of Barnabas, or a translation based on the Latin . . . a sense unknown to antiquity, but now common among the people of Greece."[1]

End Note:

1. James Donaldson, *The Apostolical Fathers: A Critical Account of their Genuine Writings and of their Doctrines*, MacMillan and Co., London, 1874, pp. 316-317.

Appendix C

Responding to Critics of Simonides

The basic claim of Simonides' production of Sinaiticus has been no secret. It was well publicized in the 1860s, particularly in England. It has recently been revived in the United States and Britain through the efforts of researchers such as J. K. Elliott, Chris Pinto, Bill Cooper, and others. Critics such as James White certainly have sought to reject the claims that Simonides produced Sinaiticus. He, along with William Aldis Wright, Henry Bradshaw, *The Guardian* newspaper, and others 150 years ago, have sought to defend the antiquity of Sinaiticus. Add Kurt Aland and virtually all relatively modern critical text editors to the list of defenders of Sinaiticus and critics of Simonides. Let us consider several of the objections that have surfaced recently, seeking to maintain the claim of antiquity for Sinaiticus.

In 1982, a scholar by the name of J. K. Elliott released a book entitled, *Codex Sinaiticus and the Simonides Affair: An examination of the nineteenth century claim that Codex Sinaiticus was not an ancient manuscript.* [1] In it, Elliot carefully and methodically laid out the claims of Simonides and then systematically attempted to discredit him. The book is primarily a record of the back and forth between Simonides, Tischendorf, and their surrogates. It is verbose and tedious. It is like watching a liberal television network or liberal newspaper bring any and all dirt or allegations it can find to discredit a conservative candidate for president. Elliott does not get into any of the forensic evidences, though they certainly were available by 1982. He also ignores the textual critiques of James Donaldson. He focuses primarily on nitpicking minutia and details of Simonides' account or that of his surrogates. It is like watching a political reporter from CNN or NBC give an "unbiased" report about George W. Bush, Donald Trump, or some other conservative candidate. Though the source of much information, Elliott's conclusions are clearly biased. He seems afraid of what his peers might think if he questioned the antiquity of Sinaiticus.

As the controversy has erupted again in recent years, others have sought to debunk Simonides. Like Elliot, they do not address the forensic evidence or the textual critique of James Donaldson. Rather, they focus on general textual issues which they claim negates Simonides' assertions. Let us consider several of these criticisms.

No Known Exemplars

One allegation is that there are no known exemplars from which Simonides could have worked. There are several simple rebuttals to that objection.

First, Simonides openly said that he worked from the Moscow Edition of both Testaments published and presented to the Greeks by the "illustrious brothers Zosimas."[2] The brothers Zosimas were

Russian Orthodox clergy who maintained contact with certain elements of the Greek Orthodox Church. The Greek Orthodox monastery at Mount Athos, St. Panteleemon, of which Simonides was connected, was a monastery in fellowship with the Russian Church. Exactly what the Moscow Edition of the Bible was, we are not further told. But quite evidently modern western scholarship has little knowledge of the textual sources in the Russian and Greek Orthodox circles.

Secondly, there presently are around 1,000 Greek manuscripts of the New Testament located at Mount Athos which have not been catalogued or analyzed by western textual experts.[3] Ironically, these same textual experts have had little interest in them because they are assumed to be of Byzantine tradition (i.e., traditional text). Moreover, the authorities at Mount Athos are not very interested in letting American textual experts get involved in analyzing their manuscripts because they know the majority of them are hostile to the Byzantine textual tradition. There is even less insight into Russian Orthodox manuscripts of the New Testament. Simonides clearly indicated that his primary source came from Moscow.

Alexandrian Text?

Another objection posed by some is that how could Simonides of the Greek Orthodox Church, which uses only Byzantine texts, produce a manuscript which seems to be of the Alexandrian textual family?

Recall that conventional wisdom holds that Sinaiticus along with Vaticanus and several other old manuscripts were of the Alexandrian textual family. That is, the presumption is they were copied in or about Alexandria, Egypt, in the fourth century. However, the conclusion that the codices Sinaiticus, Vaticanus, Bezae, and Alexandrinus are all Alexandrian is a highly subjective opinion. The so-called Alexandrian textual family is highly amorphous and disparate to put it mildly. The analysis of paleography is a particularly subjective craft and certainly is not objective science. In other words, it is principally the opinion of one paleographer versus another.

Though there is general agreement that Vaticanus was initially produced in Alexandria, it is dissimilar in its textual variations when compared to Sinaiticus. Dean Burgon, a conservative, Bible-believing textual expert of the 19th century wrote an entire book on the disparate differences between Sinaiticus and Vaticanus. As you read his quote below, recall that one of the names of Vaticanus was "B" and Sinaiticus is also called "aleph."

He wrote,

> "It matters nothing that they are discovered on careful scrutiny to differ essentially, not only from ninety-nine out of a hundred of the whole body of extant MSS. besides, but even from one another. In the gospels alone B (Vaticanus) is found to omit at least 2877 words: to add 536, to substitute, 935; to transpose, 2098: to modify 1132 (in all 7578): - the corresponding figures for Aleph being 3455 omitted, 839 added, 1114 substituted, 2299 transposed, 1265 modified (in all 8972). And be it remembered that the omissions, additions, substitutions, transpositions, and modifications, are by

> no means the same in both. It is in fact easier to find two consecutive verses in which these two mss. differ the one from the other, than two consecutive verses in which they entirely agree."[4]

Burgon went on to write,

> "In the Gospels alone Vaticanus has 589 readings quite peculiar to itself, affecting 858 words while Aleph has 1460 such readings, affecting 2640 words."[5]

As noted earlier in this volume, these two manuscripts, which again would become the principal pillars of the modern Critical Text, are dissimilar to such a degree that they could be collated into one text borders on the absurd. The two differ in thousands of places.

That being said, however, there is a similar pattern of omissions of verses or phrases in Sinaiticus which parallels that of Vaticanus, when compared to the traditional text. For example in both Vaticanus and Sinaiticus, Matthew 12:47, 16:2b-3, 17:21, 18:11, and 23:14 are omitted. The pattern of omissions in Mark are similar between Sinaiticus and Vaticanus. There are similar parallels in other New Testament omissions, though the omissions in Sinaiticus and Vaticanus are certainly not identical. A case might thus be made that they are of the same textual family — Alexandrian.

We really don't know the provenance of Sinaiticus, according to *conventional* history. But Dr. Simonides did assert that he copied from the Moscow Edition.[6] It would seem that the text of the Moscow Edition of the Greek New Testament is similar to that of Vaticanus and thus arguably Alexandrian. It apparently was in the library of St. Panteleemon at Mount Athos at that time just as Vaticanus was in the library of the Vatican. They evidently were of the same textual origins, originating in Alexandra once upon a time.

Moreover, the fifth-century Alexandrian manuscript called Codex Alexandrinus was actually located at Mount Athos before being transported to the British Museum where it currently is housed.[7] Though Alexandrinus apparently had nothing to do with the production of Sinaiticus, it is proof positive that Alexandrian manuscripts have been located at Mount Athos. Thus, the objection that Sinaiticus is an Alexandrian type of manuscript as a means of negating it coming out of Mount Athos evaporates.

Sinaiticus was Written by Several Different Scribes

The allegation is that the handwriting of several different scribes are apparent in Sinaiticus thus disproving Simonides' claim that he was the penman thereof. The argument once again is that the claims of Simonides are thus false.

The answer to this objection is simple. First, we once again touch upon the opinion of paleographers. As noted before, paleography is quite subjective and hardly definitive. But, we concede this point and agree that there were several different scribes whose handwriting is discernible in Sinaiticus.

However, and secondly, the simple fact is that Simonides from the outset noted that he was assisted by the staff calligrapher of St. Panteleemon by the name of Dionysius. He was not the principal scribe; Simonides was. But he did assist in the overall project. Moreover, Simonides' uncle Benedict also assisted, particularly in editing and correcting errors. Simonides worked in some haste and there thus were not a few scribal errors. His uncle thereafter went back and noted throughout the manuscript those errors and worked at correcting them. It was for this cause the project was never presented as a gift to the Tsar of Russia. It needed to be recopied which it never was.

Simonides said as much.

> "Of the internal evidence of the MS. I shall not now speak. Any person learned in palaeography ought to be able to tell at once that it is a MS. of the present age. But I may just note that my uncle Benedict corrected the MS in many places, and as it was intended to be re-copied, he marked many letters which he purposed to have illuminated. The corrections in the handwriting of my uncle I can, of course, point out as also those of Dionysius the calligraphist. In various places I marked in the margin the initials of the different MSS from which I had taken certain passages and readings."[8]

Thus the objection of the handwriting of several different scribes in Sinaiticus does not negate Simonides' claim. To the contrary, it validates it. He was the principle scribe. The staff calligrapher of the monastery assisted in the project and his uncle Benedict made copious corrections and marginal notes. And that is exactly what is evident upon examining Sinaiticus, even today.

Sinaiticus was Corrected by Multiple Correctors

In light of the previous objection and its answer, this objection is specious. The premise is that Simonides was supposedly the sole worker on the project. The allegation thus is that there are several who made corrections. Therefore, Simonides is devious and dishonest.

Once again, the subjectivity of paleography arises. But, we will once more cede the point. However, as noted in the quote from Simonides above, he freely noted that the staff calligrapher of the monastery, Dionysius, and his uncle Benedict were both involved in making corrections. Rather than disproving Simonides' claim, this objection once again confirms its validity. Moreover, Kallinokos, Simonides' associate, wrote that a man by the name of Callistratus was involved in the correcting of the codex along with the others mentioned above. This was published in *The Literary Churchman* newspaper of December 16, 1862.

Simonides did not have Time to Accomplish the Task

This allegation presumes that Simonides could not have accomplished the task of producing Sinaiticus from 1839 until the latter part of 1840. The assumption is that it would take years to accomplish such a task.

However, this objection collapses when other historical information is considered. When Tischendorf was negotiating with the Vatican for access to Vaticanus, he was allowed access to Vaticanus for fourteen days and for three hours each day in 1866. Frederic Kenyon, a textual historian friendly to the critical text and the antiquity of Sinaiticus wrote, "By making the most of his time Tischendorf was able in 1867 to publish the most perfect edition of the manuscript which had yet appeared."[9] If Tischendorf could copy the New Testament of Vaticanus in 42 hours, surely Simonides could have copied the entire Bible in a period longer than one year.

Furthermore, Desiderius Erasmus was the first to place the Greek New Testament into print. He arrived at Basel, Switzerland in July of 1515 to collate and prepare the master manuscript for the printers to work from. The printing began on October 2, 1515 and was released on March 1, 1516. That is about five months from start to finish. To be sure, Erasmus first edition was hurried, but he did it in less than six months.

The final nail in the coffin of this objection is the work of Tischendorf himself. Upon finally absconding from Sinai with the remainder of what would be called Sinaiticus, Tischendorf copied Vaticanus in two months, March and April of 1859, at Cairo, Egypt. This amounted to 110,000 lines of text. He did have assistance of two other German scribes, but Simonides also had help and it took him over a year to copy Sinaiticus which is of comparable length. The claim that Simonides did not have enough time to copy Sinaiticus is false on its face.

Simonides was an accomplished calligrapher and paleographer. Greek was his native language. The objection that he would not have time to simply copy what came to be known as Sinaiticus in what was greater than one year simply does not hold water. And, recall that he did not do the project alone, but was assisted by Dionysius the staff calligrapher of the monastery.

Conclusion

There have been seemingly endless attacks against the credibility of Simonides. Every possible device to discredit or undercut his claim of producing Sinaiticus has been attempted. It continues to this day, more than 150 years later. But every objection can and has been refuted.

The stakes are high. If Simonides' claim is true, then Sinaiticus is not one of the oldest Bibles in existence, but is rather a hastily done codex produced in 1840 and later made to appear ancient. To this day, Sinaiticus is one of the principal pillars of the modern critical text whence virtually all modern Bible translations are based. Academic prestige is on the line. Intellectual pride is on the line. And, vast amounts of money have been invested in modern translations of the Bible based upon the assumption that Sinaiticus and its colleague Vaticanus are the oldest and best manuscripts. For the liberal textual establishment, Sinaiticus must be propped up at all costs. But it is a fraud — not in what Simonides did, but in what others did to give it the appearance of age and pawn it off on that basis.

End Notes:

1. J. K. Elliott, *Codex Sinaiticus and the Simonides Affair: An examination of the nineteenth century claim that Codex Sinaiticus was not an ancient manuscript*, Patriarchal Institute for Patristic Studies, Thessalonica, Greece, 1982.

2. *The Literary Churchman* 16th December, 1862, and *The Journal of Sacred Literature*, October 1862.

3. David Brown, Ph.D., President of the King James Bible Research Council, Oak Creek, Wisconsin.

4. John Burgon, *The Revision Revised*, Original publisher unknown, 1883. Reprint, Collinswood, N.J. Dean Burgon Society, n.d., p. 11.

5. Ibid., p. 319.

6. Once again, little if anything is known of the provenance of the Moscow Edition.

7. F. C. Burkitt, *Codex Alexandrinus*, Journal of Theological Studies XI, (1909-1910), pp. 603-606.

8. *The Guardian* September 3, 1862.

9. Frederic Kenyon, *Our Bible and the Ancient Manuscripts*, 4th ed. (New York: Harper Bros., 1895) pp. 138-9.

Appendix D

Verses deleted in Vaticanus compared to the Traditional Text

The text of Vaticanus has omitted many verses from the Traditional Text

Matthew 12:47 "~~Then one said unto him, Behold, thy mother and thy brethren stand without, desiring to speak with thee~~."

16:2b-3 "~~When it is evening, ye say, It will be fair weather: for the sky is red. 3 And in the morning, It will be foul weather to day: for the sky is red and lowring. O ye hypocrites, ye can discern the face of the sky; but can ye not discern the signs of the times?~~"

Matthew 17:21 "~~Howbeit this kind goeth not out but by prayer and fasting~~."

Matthew 18:11 "~~For the Son of man is come to save that which was lost~~."

Matthew 23:14 "~~Woe unto you, scribes and Pharisees, hypocrites! for ye devour widows' houses, and for a pretence make long prayer: therefore ye shall receive the greater damnation~~."

Mark 7:16 "~~If any man have ears to hear, let him hear~~."

Mark 9:44 "~~Where their worm dieth not, and the fire is not quenched~~."

Mark 9:46 "~~Where their worm dieth not, and the fire is not quenched~~."

Mark 11:26 "~~But if ye do not forgive, neither will your Father which is in heaven forgive your trespasses~~."

Mark 15:28 "~~And the scripture was fulfilled, which saith, And he was numbered with the transgressors~~."

Mark 16:9–20 "~~Now when Jesus was risen early the first day of the week, he appeared first to Mary Magdalene, out of whom he had cast seven devils.~~
~~10 And she went and told them that had been with him, as they mourned and wept.~~
~~11 And they, when they had heard that he was alive, and had been seen of her, believed not.~~
~~12 After that he appeared in another form unto two of them, as they walked, and went into the country.~~
~~13 And they went and told it unto the residue: neither believed they them.~~

~~14 Afterward he appeared unto the eleven as they sat at meat, and upbraided them with their unbelief and hardness of heart, because they believed not them which had seen him after he was risen.~~
~~15 And he said unto them, Go ye into all the world, and preach the gospel to every creature.~~
~~16 He that believeth and is baptized shall be saved; but he that believeth not shall be damned.~~
~~17 And these signs shall follow them that believe; In my name shall they cast out devils; they shall speak with new tongues;~~
~~18 They shall take up serpents; and if they drink any deadly thing, it shall not hurt them; they shall lay hands on the sick, and they shall recover.~~
~~19 So then after the Lord had spoken unto them, he was received up into heaven, and sat on the right hand of God.~~
~~20 And they went forth, and preached every where, the Lord working with them, and confirming the word with signs following. Amen~~.

> The Book of Mark ends with verse 16:8. (The end of Mark in Vaticanus contains an empty column after Verse 16:8, indicating the scribe intentionally omitted it. It is the only empty New Testament column in the Codex.)

Luke 17:36 "~~Two men shall be in the field; the one shall be taken, and the other left~~."

Luke 22:43–44 "~~And there appeared an angel unto him from heaven, strengthening him.~~

~~44 And being in an agony he prayed more earnestly: and his sweat was as it were great drops of blood falling down to the ground~~."

John 5:4 "~~For an angel went down at a certain season into the pool, and troubled the water: whosoever then first after the troubling of the water stepped in was made whole of whatsoever disease he had~~."

John 7:53–8:11 "~~And every man went unto his own house.~~
~~1 Jesus went unto the mount of Olives.~~
~~2 And early in the morning he came again into the temple, and all the people came unto him; and he sat down, and taught them.~~
~~3 And the scribes and Pharisees brought unto him a woman taken in adultery; and when they had set her in the midst,~~
~~4 They say unto him, Master, this woman was taken in adultery, in the very act.~~
~~5 Now Moses in the law commanded us, that such should be stoned: but what sayest thou?~~
~~6 This they said, tempting him, that they might have to accuse him. But Jesus stooped down, and with his finger wrote on the ground, as though he heard them not.~~
~~7 So when they continued asking him, he lifted up himself, and said unto them, He that is without sin among you, let him first cast a stone at her.~~
~~8 And again he stooped down, and wrote on the ground.~~
~~9 And they which heard it, being convicted by their own conscience, went out one by one, beginning at the eldest, even unto the last: and Jesus was left alone, and the woman standing in the midst.~~
~~10 When Jesus had lifted up himself, and saw none but the woman, he said unto her, Woman, where are those thine accusers? hath no man condemned thee?~~

~~11 She said, No man, Lord. And Jesus said unto her, Neither do I condemn thee: go, and sin no more~~."

Acts 8:37 "~~And Philip said, If thou believest with all thine heart, thou mayest. And he answered and said, I believe that Jesus Christ is the Son of God~~."

Acts 15:34 "~~Notwithstanding it pleased Silas to abide there still~~."

Acts 24:7 "~~But the chief captain Lysias came upon us, and with great violence took him away out of our hands~~."

Acts 28:29 "~~And when he had said these words, the Jews departed, and had great reasoning among themselves~~."

Romans 16:24 "~~The grace of our Lord Jesus Christ be with you all. Amen~~."

1 Peter 5:3 "~~Neither as being lords over God's heritage, but being ensamples to the flock~~."

Some of the phrases of verses not found in Vaticanus but in the Traditional Text

Matthew 5:44 – εὐλογε?τε τοὺς καταρωμένους ὑμ?ς, καλ?ς ποιε?τε το?ς μισο?σιν ὑμ?ς ("~~bless them who curse you, do good to them who despitefully use you and persecute you~~").

Matthew 10:37b – καὶ ὁ φιλ?ν υἱὸν ἢ θυγατέρα ὑπὲρ ἐμὲ οὐκ ἔστιν μου ἄξιος (“~~and he that loveth son or daughter more than me is not worthy of me~~”).

Matthew 15:6 – ἢ τὴν μητέρα (αὐτο?) (“~~or his mother~~”).

Matthew 20:23 – καὶ τὸ βάπτισμα ὃ ἐγὼ βαπτίζομαι βαπτισθήσεσθε (“~~and be baptized with the baptism that I am baptized with~~”).

Mark 10:7 – καὶ προσκολληθήσεται πρὸς τὴν γυνα?κα αὐτο? (“~~and cleave to his wife~~”).

Mark 10:19 – μη αποστερησης omitted (“~~Defraud not~~”).

Luke 9:55–56 – και ειπεν, Ουκ οιδατε ποιου πνευματος εστε υμεις; ο γαρ υιος του ανθρωπου ουκ ηλθεν ψυχας ανθρωπων απολεσαι αλλα σωσαι (and He said: “~~Ye know not what manner of spirit ye are of.~~
~~56 For the Son of man is not come to destroy men’s lives, but to save them~~”).

Luke 11:4 – αλλα ρυσαι ημας απο του πονηρου (“~~but deliver us from evil~~”).

Luke 23:34 – ‘ο δε ιησου□ ελεγεν πατερ αφε□ αυτοι□ ου γαρ οιδασιν τι ποιουσιν (“~~Then said Jesus, Father, forgive them; for they know not what they do.~~”)

Bibliography

Aland, Kurt and Barbara, *The Text of the New Testament*, translated by Erroll F. Rhodes, Grand Rapids: Eerdmans, 1989.

Burgon, John. *The Revision Revised*, Original publisher unknown, 1883. Reprint, Collinswood, N.J.: Dean Burgon Society, n.d.

Burgon, John. *Inspiration and Interpretation.* London: J. H. & Jas. Parker, 1861. reprint, Collinswood, Jersey: Bible for Today, 1984.

Burgon, John. *The Revision Revised.* London: John Murray, Albemarle Street, 1883.

Burkitt, F. C. *Codex Alexandrinus*. Journal of Theological Studies XI, 1909-1910.

Codex Sinaiticus: Facsimile Greek Edition, Peabody, Massachusetts: Hendrickson Publishers, 2011. ISBN 159856577X

Cooper, Bill. *The Forging of Codex Sinaiticus,* Kindle edition, 2016, location 669.

Dobschutz, Ernst. New York: *Hastings Encyclopaedia of Religion and Ethics*. Vol. 2., 1910.

Donaldson, James. *The Apostolical Fathers: A critical Account of their Genuine Writings and of their Doctrines*. London: MacMillan and Co., 1874.

Dressel, Albrecht. *Patrum Apostolicorum Opera*. Leipzig: J. C.Hinrichs – Bibliopola1863.

Elliott, J.K. *Codex Sinaiticus and the Simonides Affair*. Thessalonki, Greece: Patriarchal Institute for Patristic Studies, 1982.

Farrer, James Anson. *Literary Forgeries*. Bombay and Callcutta: Longmans, Green & Co., 1907.

Harris, James Rendel. *Stichometry.* London:1893.

Harvard Theological Review 68, 1975, pp. 17-33.

Hills, Edward. *The King James Version Defended.* Des Moines: Christian Research Press, 1956.

Lambros, Spyridon Paulou. *Catalogue of the Greek Manuscripts on Mount Athos*. (2 vols). London: Cambridge University Press, 1895.

Lambrou, Michael. "Re: [HM] Archimedes Palimpsest," Internet message at http://sunsite.utk.edu/math archives/,http/hypennail/ historia/jul99/0034,html, 3.

Lucas, Arthur. *Forensic Chemistry*., London: E. Arnold & Company, 1921.

M'Clymont, J. A. *New Testament Criticism: Its History and Results*. London: Hodder & Stoughton, 1913.

Madan, Falconer. *Books in Manuscript*, London: Edward Arnold & Company, 1920 (rev. ed.).

Metzger, Bruce M. *Manuscripts of the Greek Bible: An Introduction to Greek Palaeography*, Oxford: Oxford University Press, 1991.

Mitchell, M.M. & Duncan PA. *Chicago's Archaic Mark (MS 2427):* "A reintroduction to its enigmas and a fresh collation of its readings." *Novum Testamentum*, Volume 48, Leipzig, 1844. (As noted by Bill Cooper in *The Forging of Codex Sinaiticus*.)

Nicolson, *Adam. God's Secretaries: The Making of the King James Bible.* London: Harper Collins, 2005.

Nolan, Frederick. *An Inquiry into the Integrity of the Greek Vulgate: or, Received Text of the New Testament*. London: F. C. & J. Rivington, 1815, 1815.

Papademetriou, Dean and Sopko, *Andrew J. The Church and the Library: Studies in Honor of Rev. Dr. George C. Papademetriou,* 2005. Boston: Somerset Hall Press, 416 Commonwealth Avenue, Suite 117, Boston, Massachusetts, 2005.

Pinto, *Chris. Tares Among the Wheat*, Adullam Films, www.adullamfilms.com, 2012.

Scrivener, Frederick Henry Ambrose. *Six Lectures on the Text of the New Testament and the Ancient Manuscripts*. London: George Bell and Sons, 1875.

Scrivener, Frederick Henry Ambrose; Edward Miller (1894). *A Plain Introduction to the Criticism of the New Testament*. 1 (4 ed.). London: George Bell & Sons.

Sevcenko, Ihor. "New Documents on Constantine Tischendorf and the Codex Sinaiticus," *Scriptorium*, vol. 18 (1964) p. 61. Reprinted in the author's *Byzantine and the Slavs in Letters and Culture* (Cambridge, Massachusetts: Harvard Ukrainian Research Institute; Napoli: Istituto Unversitario Orientalie, 1991).

Simonides, Constantine. Η πρους τους εξ Εβραινων πιστους επιστολη αποστολικου πατρος ημων Βαρναβα. [Σμθρνα]. Smyrna, Turkey: Star of the East, 1843. (Roughly translated:

Simonides, Constantine. The production on parchment of the faithful apostolic letter of our Father Barnabas, 1843.)

Skeat, T. C. "The Codex Sinaiticus, the Codex Vaticanus and Constantine," Oxford: Journal of Theological Studies 50 (1999),

Sorenson, *David. Touch Not the Unclean Thing.* Duluth, Minn.: Northstar Ministries, 2001.

Sorenson, David. *God's Perfect Book.* Duluth, Minn.: Northstar Ministries, 2009.

Stewart, Charles. *A Biographical Memoir of Constantine Simonides, Dr. ph., of Stageira, with a Brief Defence of the Authenticity of his Manuscripts*. London: C.J. Skeet, 1859.

The Guardian newspaper, London: September 3, 1862. Cited by Elliott.

The Athenaeum. London: 8th January 1876.

The Literary Churchman, London: 16th December, 1862.

The Journal of Sacred Literature, England: October 1862.

The Saturday Review, London: January 2, 1875.

Tischendorf, Constantine. *Novum Testamentum Graece, Volumen III*, Prolegomena scripsit Leipzig, Germany: Casparus Renatus Gregory, 1884.

Tischendorf, Constantine. *When were our Gospels Written?* 150 Nassau Street, New York, New York: American Tact Society, 1867.

Tischendorf, Constantine. *Novum Testamentum Vaticanum. Post Angeli Maii Aloirumque Imperfectos Labores ex ipso Codice.* Leipzig, Germanuy: University of Leipzig, 1867.

Uspensky, Porphyry. *The First Trip to the Sinai Monastery in 1845*. St. Petersburg, Russia, 1856.

Wikipedia: https://en.wikipedia.org/wiki/Codex_Vaticanus, 2016, 115-117.

Yoonan, Paul D. *History of the Peshitta*, 06/01/2000 http://www.peshitta.org/initial/peshitta.html.

Bibliography

Index